THE ILLUSTRATED
WOODY ALLEN
READER

Edited by Linda Sunshine

JONATHAN CAPE

LONDON

First Published in the United Kingdom 1993

10 9 8 7 6 5 4 3 2 1

© 1993 Woody Allen and Linda Sunshine

Woody Allen and Linda Sunshine have asserted their rights under the Copyright, Designs and Patents Act, 1988 to be identified as the authors of this work.

First published in the United Kingdom in 1993 by Jonathan Cape
Random House, 20 Vauxhall Bridge Road, London SW1V 2SA

Random House Australia (Pty) Limited
20 Alfred Street, Milsons Point Sydney
New South Wales 2061, Australia

Random House New Zealand Limited
18 Poland Road, Glenfield
Auckland 10, New Zealand

Random House South Africa (Pty) Limited
PO Box 337, Bergvlei, South Africa

Random House UK Ltd Reg. No. 954009

A CIP catalogue record for this book
is available from the British Library

ISBN 0-224-03825-7

Manufactured in the United States of America

Designed by Nai Y. Chang

Contents

INTRODUCTION

You Should Know That About Me

Woody Allen's First Recorded Monologue, March, 1964

Since I was here last, a lot of significant things have occurred in my private life that I thought we could go over tonight and, um, evaluate. I moved. Let me start right at the very beginning. I formerly lived in Manhattan, uptown, east, in a brownstone building but I was constantly getting mugged and assaulted and sadistically beaten about the face and neck. So I moved into a doorman apartment house on Park Avenue that's rich and secure and expensive and great. I lived there for two weeks and my doorman attacked me.

I don't know what else is happening. Oh, I know, I became a corporation since I was here last time. Last year, I had difficulty with my income tax. I tried to take my analyst off as a business deduction, you know, and the government said that it was entertainment. We compromised finally and made it a religious contribution.

I formed a corporation this year. I'm the president, my mother's vice-president, my father's secretary and my grandmother is treasurer. My uncle is on the Board of Directors. They got together and they tried to squeeze me out. I formed a power bloc with my uncle and we sent my grandmother to jail.

I went to NYU, myself, I was a philosophy major. I took all the abstract philosophy courses in college like Truth and Beauty and Advanced Truth and Beauty and Intermediate Truth and Introduction to God. Death 101. I was thrown out of NYU my freshman year. I cheated on my metaphysical final in college. I looked within the soul of the boy sitting next to me.

They threw me out and my mother, who is really a

sensitive woman, locked herself in the bathroom and took an overdose of Mah-Jongg tiles.

I was in analysis—you should know that about me—I was in group analysis when I was younger because I couldn't afford private. I was captain of the Latent Paranoid softball team. We used to play all the neurotics on Sunday morning. Nail biters against the bedwetters. And if you've never seen neurotics play softball, it's really funny. I used to steal second base and feel guilty and go back.

Also, I have a boy cousin that my parents loved more than me that really destroyed me. I have a boy cousin that went through four years of college and became a mutual fund sales-man. And he married a very thin girl from the neighborhood who had her nose lifted by a golf pro. You know, hit it and it just hooked up over her head.

And they moved to the suburbs and they have all kinds of status symbols. They have their own home and a station wagon and fire insurance and life insurance and mutual funds and his wife has orgasmic insurance. If her husband fails to satisfy her sexually, Mutual of Omaha has to pay her every month.

I don't know what else to tell you about myself. I, uh, I was a writer and an actor. I was a television writer. I was not an actor. I was in acting class. We did a play in acting class by Paddy Chayefsky called *Gideon* and I played the part of God in *Gideon*. And it was method acting, so two weeks beforehand I started to live the part offstage. I really came on Godly. I was really fabulous. I put on a blue suit. I took taxicabs all over New York. I tipped big because He would have. I got into a fight with a guy and I forgave him. It's true. Some guy hit my fender and I said unto him, "Be fruitful and multiply." But not in those words.

Monologue

The Final Scene from *Husbands and Wives,* 1992

Interviewer: So what's your life like now?

Gabe: I'm out of the race at the moment. I don't want to get involved. I don't want to hurt anyone, or to get hurt. I don't mind living by myself and working. It's temporary. The urge will pass. Then I'll want to get back into the swing of things. That's how it goes. But as I say I'm working on a new novel. Not the old one anymore. It's fine, absolutely fine.

Interviewer: Is it different?

Gabe: My novel? Yes, it's less confessional, more political. Can I go? Is it over?

Husbands and Wives

CHAPTER ONE

My Parents' Values: God and Carpeting

Annie Hall

used to sit in the dumb row in school, you know. Vegetable mentality. I made friends with him years later, when we got older. I removed a thorn from his paw.

Once I was on my way for my violin lesson when I was a kid. I'm walking past the pool room and Floyd and all his friends are out, you know. They're swiping hub caps in Brooklyn—from moving cars.

I walked past and he yelled out to me, "Hey, Red!"

I was a cocky kid. Put down my violin. I go up to him. I say, "My name is not Red. If you want me, call me by my regular name. It's Master Heywood Allen."

I spent that winter in a wheelchair. A team of doctors labored to remove a violin. Lucky it wasn't a cello.

I'm not a fighter. I have bad reflexes and I can't fight. I was once run over by a car with a flat tire being pushed by two guys.

Monologue

A Precocious Child

He had been a precocious child. An intellectual. At twelve, he had translated the poems of T. S. Eliot into English, after some vandals had broken into the library and translated them into French. And as if his I.Q. did not isolate him enough, he suffered untold injustices and persecutions because of his religion, mostly from his parents. True, the old man was a member of the synagogue, and his mother too, but they could never accept the fact that their son was Jewish. "How did it happen?" his father asked, bewildered. My face looks Semitic, Weinstein thought every morning as he shaved. He had been mistaken several times for Robert Redford, but on each occasion it was by a blind person.

"No Kaddish for Weinstein"

Seth Green, *Radio Days.*

Charles Riggs III and
Geoffrey Riggs, *Stardust
Memories*.

Where Did You Learn About Sex?

Luna: Where did you learn about sex?

Miles: Me? From my mother. When I was a little kid I asked
her where babies came from. And she thought I said
rabies. She said from a dog bite. And a week later a
lady on the block gave birth to triplets. I thought she
was bitten by a Great Dane.

Sleeper

He Was the Son of . . .

Narrator: Who was this Leonard Zelig that seemed to create
such diverse impressions everywhere?

All that was known of him was that he was the son of a
Yiddish actor named Morris Zelig, whose performance as
Puck in the Orthodox version of *A Midsummer Night's Dream*
was coolly received.

The elder Zelig's second marriage is marked by constant
violent quarreling, so much so that although the family lives
over a bowling alley, it is the bowling alley that complains of
noise.

As a boy, Leonard Zelig is frequently bullied by anti-
Semites. His parents, who never take his part and blame him
for everything, side with the anti-Semites.

They punish him often by locking him in a dark closet.
When they are really angry, they get into the closet with him.

From *The Passionate Collector*

On his deathbed, Morris Zelig tells his son that his life is a meaningless nightmare of suffering, and the only advice he gives him is to save string.

Zelig

He Had So Many Good Qualities

Narrator: Mr. and Mrs. Starkwell are ashamed of their son's criminal record and so wear disguises. . . .

Mom: He had so many good qualities. . . .

Dad: Yeah, name—name 'em.

Mom: He had all sorts of mechanical abilities. He was artistic. . . . Do you remember the painting he did for your birthday?

Dad: Artistic? No-good atheist is what he was. That's what he was. I used to hit him and try to teach him about God, but would he listen? No.

Take the Money and Run

Take the Money and Run

I guess I had a good relationship with my parents. They very rarely hit . . . I think they hit me once, actually, in my whole childhood. They started beating me on the twenty-third of December, 1942, and stopped beating me in the late spring of forty-four.

Bananas

My Mother and Father Could Find an Argument in Any Subject

Joe: And then there were my mother and father . . . two people who could find an argument in any subject.

Father: Wait a minute! Are you telling me you think the Atlantic is a greater ocean than the Pacific?

Mother: No. Have it your way. The Pacific is greater.

Joe: I mean, how many people can fight over oceans?! . . .

Host *(on radio):* And now, the makers of General Sparkplugs present "The Court of Human Emotions" with that renowned counselor of the human heart, Thomas Abercrombie.

23

Joe: My parents loved the show where ordinary people's problems were solved . . . I found the show silly. I imagined my parents on it, airing their usual complaints.

Mother: He's a business failure. We're forced to live with my relations. I could've married Sol Slotkin.

Father: He's dead.

Mother: While he was alive, he was working.

Father: She's lost without her family around her. They're like Huns! If I'd married a more encouraging woman . . .

Mother: So, who's right?

Mr. Abercrombie: I think you both deserve each other.

Mother: What does he mean by that?

Father: We didn't come here to be insulted.

Mother: I love him, but what did I do to deserve him?

Radio Days

Throw the Kid Out

I was kidnapped once. I was standing in front of my schoolyard and a black sedan pulls up. Two guys get out and they ask me if I want to go away with them to a land where everybody is fairies and elves and I could have all the comic books I want and chocolate and wax lips, you know, and I said yes. I got into the car with them because I figured, you know, what the hell, I was home that week from college anyhow.

They drive me off and send a ransom note to my parents. My father has bad reading habits, so he gets into bed at night with the ransom note and he reads half of it, you know, and he gets drowsy and falls asleep. Then he lent it out.

Meanwhile, they take me to a house in New Jersey, bound and gagged.

My parents finally realized that I'm kidnapped and they snap into action immediately. They rent out my room.

The ransom note says for my father to leave a thousand dollars in a hollow tree in New Jersey. He has no trouble raising the thousand dollars but he gets a hernia carrying the hollow tree.

The F.B.I. surround the house. "Throw the kid out," they say. "Give us your guns and come out with your hands up."

The kidnappers say, "We'll throw the kid out but let us

keep our guns and get to our car."

The F.B.I. says, "Throw the kid out. We'll let you get to your car but give us your guns."

The kidnappers say, "We'll throw the kid out but let us keep our guns. We don't have to get to our car."

The F.B.I. says, "Keep the kid."

The F.B.I. decides to lob in tear gas but they don't have tear gas so several of the agents put on the death scene from *Camille.*

Tear-stricken, my abductors give themselves up. They're sentenced to fifteen years on a chain gang and they escape—twelve of them chained together at the ankle—getting by the guard posing as an immense charm bracelet.

Monologue

Take the Money and Run

Peter Lorre and Humphrey
Bogart, *The Maltese Falcon*,
1941.

I Identified with Peter Lorre

The first Humphrey Bogart movie I saw was *The Maltese
Falcon*. I was ten years old and I identified immediately with
Peter Lorre. The impulse to be a sniveling, effeminate, greasy
little weasel appealed to me enormously and, setting my sights
on a life of mealymouthed degradation and crime, I rapidly
achieved a reputation that caused neighboring parents to
appear at my doorstep carrying torches, a large rope, and bags
of quicklime.

Life magazine

I Grew to Full Manhood

I grew to full manhood . . . actually, five foot six, which is
technically not full manhood in Russia but you can still own
property. Over five three you can own land. Under five three
you need special permission from the Czar.

Love and Death

My Sister Married Money

I had a sister and two brothers. Jenny married money. Not an
actual human being—it was a pile of singles. My brother Vic
got in with a gang of plagiarists. He was in the middle of sign-
ing his name to "The Waste Land" when the feds surrounded
the house. He got ten years. Some rich kid from a highfalutin'
family who signed Pound's "Cantos" got off on probation.
That's the law for you. Charlie—that's my younger brother—
he's been a numbers runner, a fence and a loan shark. Never
could find himself. Eventually, he was arrested for loitering.
He loitered for seven years, till he realized it was not the kind
of crime that brought in any money.

"Confessions of a Burglar"

Mother: Ah, gosh, didn't Bea look lovely?
Father: What did she do? Fall into a vat of perfume?
Mother: You know when we were younger, of the three sis-
        ters, she used to be considered the pretty one.
Father: Some contest.

Radio Days

Call Your Mother

On her deathbed, O'Shawn's mother Bridget begged her son to
abandon poetry and become a vacuum-cleaner salesman.
O'Shawn couldn't promise and suffered from anxiety and guilt
the rest of his life, although at the International Poetry
Convention in Geneva, he sold W. H. Auden and Wallace
Stevens each a Hoover.

"The Irish Genius"

WOODY ALLEN (Alan Felix) is the son of a Latvian Prince.
He came to the United States as a result of a Pogrom at which
he was the only one who showed up. . . . He played Willie
Loman in *Mr. Roberts* to the consternation of many around
him.

Playbill magazine

Oh, Mom, You Were So Charming

Alice: When dad died, you drank yourself to death with Margaritas.

Mom: I couldn't help it, darling. You know I could never resist the taste of salt around the rim of a glass.

Alice: Oh, Mom, you were so charming but so misguided. Why didn't I see it?

Mom: When it came to me and your dad, you had stars in your eyes.

Alice

His Mother Refused to Seat Him

Out on the street, he decided to go to La Coupole for a brandy. He liked La Coupole because it was always bright and crowded, and he could usually get a table—quite a difference from his own apartment where his mother, who lived there too, always refused to seat him. But tonight La Coupole was filled. Who are these faces, Cloquet wondered. They seem to blur into an abstraction: "The People." But there are no people, he thought—only individuals. Cloquet felt this was a brilliant perception, one that he could use impressively at some chic dinner party. Because of observations such as this, he had not been invited to a social gathering of any sort since 1931.

"The Condemned"

Broadway Danny Rose

Madonna and Dennis Vestunis, *Shadows and Fog.*

Lovborg's Revenge on His Mother

[Writing the character of] Mrs. Sanstad was Lovborg's revenge
on his mother. Also a critical woman, she began life as a
trapeze artist with the circus; his father, Nils Lovborg, was the
human cannonball. The two met in midair and were married
before touching ground. Bitterness slowly crept into the marriage, and by the time Lovborg was six years old, his parents
exchanged gunfire daily. This atmosphere took its toll on a
sensitive youngster like Jorgen, and soon he began to suffer
the first of his famous "moods" and "anxieties," rendering
him for some years unable to pass a roast chicken without tip-
ping his hat. In later years, he told friends that he was tense
all during the writing of *Mellow Pears* and on several occasions believed he heard his mother's voice asking him direc-
tions to Staten Island.

"Lovborg's Women Considered"

29

My Mother Went Crazy with Name Tags

Carol: Hey—you got name tags on all your underwear.
Victor: This is my first time away from home. My mother went
        crazy with name tags. They're on all my shirts and
        pants.
Carol: She shouldn't have sewn them on the outside though.

What's New Pussycat?

My Mother's Favorite Poem

Marion: The incident with Claire had left me edgy and
uncomfortable. I thought if I read for a while it might relax me.
I thumbed through my mother's edition of Rilke.

When I was sixteen, I had done a paper on his poem
about the panther and on the image that the panther saw as it
stared out from its cage. And that image I concluded could
only be death. Then I saw my mother's favorite poem,
"Archaic Torso of Apollo." There were stains on the page,
which I believe were her tears. They fell across the last line:
"For here there is no place that does not see you. You must
change your life."

Another Woman

Gabe: How'd you get the name Rain?
Rain: My parents named me after Rilke. It's my mother's
        favorite poet. So that's how I got it.

Husbands and Wives

The Heart of the Old World

My parents are what you would call, Old World. My parents
come from Brooklyn, which is the heart of the Old World.
They're very stable, down-to-earth people who don't approve
of divorce. Their values in life are God and carpeting.

I came home on a Sunday, this was a long time ago. My
father's watching the "Ed Sullivan Show" on television. He's
watching the Indiana Home for the Criminally Insane Glee
Club on the "Ed Sullivan Show."

Manhattan

My mother's in the corner knitting a chicken.

And I said I had to get a divorce. My mother put down her knitting. She got up and she went over to the furnace. She opened the door and she got in. Took it rather badly I thought.

Monologue

My Dad Was Always on the Run

My dad was always on the run from the cops and I never saw him out of disguise till I was twenty-two. For years, I thought he was a short, bearded man with dark glasses and a limp; actually, he was tall and blond and resembled Lindbergh. He was a professional bank robber, but sixty-five was the mandatory retirement age, so he had to get out. Spent his last few years in mail fraud, but the postal rates went up and he lost everything.

Mom was wanted, too. Of course, in those days it wasn't the way it is now, with women demanding equal rights and all.

Back then, if a woman turned to crime the only opportunities open to her were blackmail and, once in a while, arson. Women were used in Chicago to drive getaway cars, but only during the drivers' strike, in 1926. Terrible strike. It lasted eight weeks, and whenever a gang pulled a job and ran out with the money they were forced to walk or take a cab.

"Confessions of a Burglar"

Dad Got Struck by Lightning

After that, of course, I was rich. First thing I did was buy my mother and father that farm they'd always talked about. They claimed they had never talked about a farm and actually wanted a car and some furs, but they gave it a try. Liked the rural life, too, although Dad got struck by lightning in the north forty and for six years afterward when asked his name could only say the word "Kleenex."

"Fine Times: An Oral Memoir"

Zelig

Is It Because I Hated My Father?

Good Lord, why am I so guilty? Is it because I hated my
father? Probably it was the veal parmigiana incident. Well,
what was it doing in his wallet? If I had listened to him, I
would be blocking hats for a living. I can hear him now: "To
block hats—that is everything." I remember his reaction
when I told him I wanted to write. "The only writing you'll do
is in collaboration with an owl." I still have no idea what he
meant. What a sad man! When my first play, *A Cyst for Gus*,
was produced at the Lyceum, he attended opening night in
tails and a gas mask.

"Selections from the Allen Notebooks"

My Father's Friends

We discussed photography (her hobby) and books. She was
currently reading, with great delight, a book of Joseph
Heller's. She found it hilarious and, laughing fetchingly as she
filled my glass, said, "God, you Jews are truly exotic." Exotic?
She should only know the Greenblatts. Or Mr. and Mrs. Milton
Sharpstein, my father's friends. Or for that matter, my cousin
Tovah. Exotic? I mean, they're nice but hardly exotic with
their endless bickering over the best way to combat indiges-
tion or how far back to sit from the television set.

"Retribution"

Relatives on My Mother's Side

Actually, I had a rather dim view of my family's physical
appearance, likening the relatives on my mother's side to
something usually cultured in a petri dish. I was very hard on
my family and we all constantly teased each other and fought,
but we were close. Indeed, a compliment had not passed
through the lips of any member during my lifetime and I suspect not since God made his covenant with Abraham.

"Retribution"

33

Irving Selbst and Hope Sacharoff, *Radio Days.*

My Aunt Rose

Danny: Look, I always tried to teach you, Lou. I've always
tried to show you that sooner or later you're gonna have to
square yourself with the big guy. Is that true? You're gonna
have to pay your dues some day. You know, you're a married
man. My Aunt Rose, take my Aunt Rose. Not a beautiful
woman at all. She looked like something you'd buy in a live
bait store. But why? She had wisdom. And she used to say, you
can't ride two horses with one behind.

Broadway Danny Rose

Josh Mostel, *Radio Days*.

Weinstein's Uncle Meyer

The Depression shattered Weinstein's Uncle Meyer, who kept
his fortune under the mattress. When the market crashed, the
government called in all mattresses, and Meyer became a
pauper overnight. All that was left for him was to jump out the
window, but he lacked the nerve and sat on a window sill of
the Flatiron Building from 1930 to 1937.

"These kids with their pot and their sex," Uncle Meyer
was fond of saying. "Do they know what it is to sit on a window sill for seven years? There you see life! Of course, everybody looks like ants. But each year Tessie—may she rest in
peace—made the Seder right out there on the ledge. The family gathered round for Passover. Oy, nephew! What's the world
coming to when they have a bomb that can kill more people
than one look at Max Rifkin's daughter?"

"No Kaddish for Weinstein"

My Grandfather Was a Very Insignificant Man

I wanted to flash this watch. I flash it all the time. It's my
antique pocket watch, and it makes me look British. I need
that for my analysis. It's a gorgeous gold pocket watch. I'm
proud of it. My grandfather, on his deathbed, sold me this
pocket watch.

My grandfather was a very insignificant man, actually. At
his funeral, his hearse followed the other cars.

It was a nice funeral, though, you would've liked it. It was
a catered funeral. It was held in a big hall with accordion
players. On the buffet table, there was a replica of the
deceased in potato salad.

Monologue

Narrator: With both parents working to make ends meet, Virgil becomes closest to his grandfather, a sixty-year-old German immigrant who takes the boy to movies and baseball games. Then tragedy strikes. At a Washington Senators' game, Virgil's grandfather is struck in the head by a foul ball. The blow causes permanent injury to his mind and he is convinced he is Kaiser Wilhelm.

Take the Money and Run

Kaiser Wilhelm II

Crimes and Misdemeanors

Mother: Hey, Martin, are you sure you want to call the baby
Ellen?
Father: Sure. In memory of your cousin Eddie.
Mother: In memory? He isn't dead yet.
Father: He should be.

Radio Days

Grammy Hall

Alvy: And I love what you're wearing.
Annie: Oh, do you? Yeah? Oh well, this tie is a present from
Grammy Hall.
Alvy: Who? Grammy Hall?
Annie: Yeah, my grammy.
Alvy: What did you do, grow up in a Norman Rockwell
painting?
Annie: Yeah, I know.
Alvy: Your grammy!
Annie: I know, it's pretty silly, isn't it?
Alvy: Jesus, my grammy . . . never gave gifts, you know.
She was too busy getting raped by Cossacks.

Annie Hall

Did My Sister Lena Call?

Enid *(into the phone):* Hello, Lena, did I get you at a bad moment? . . . Every time I call you're running out. How's Julian? . . . Really? . . . Really? My God, that's a big cyst. Can he sit down? . . . Max is doing okay too—in case you're interested. . . . Fine, he has some very promising irons in the fire. . . . Listen, I won't take much of your time. I wanted to discuss the possibility of your investing in a little business venture. . . . No, no, Lena, wait, this one is much less complicated. I admit the whole greeting card thing sounded easy but when push came to shove it was a nightmare. Who knew you had to keep books and records. . . .

Lena, I-I, to be perfectly frank, we're a little strapped at the moment. . . . And how much longer can I stand on my feet selling hosiery? My ankles swell up. . . . Is that what I have to look forward to for the rest of my life?

Lena, hear me out. . . . I have two ideas. One is personalized matchbooks and the other is tropical fish—I'm talking strictly mail order. . . . Naturally, just the matchbooks— you can't put guppies in envelopes. . . .

Lena, no one's asking you to subsidize us. I know you're a dry well—believe me, I described you to someone just the other day as a dry well. . . .

Okay, Lena, it's almost seven-thirty, I gotta get the subway or I'll be late for work but I mean to follow this up. If you'd return my calls. . . . *(She hangs up.)* The woman has never forgiven me to this day for her physical appearance. Like it's my fault.

The Floating Lightbulb

My Brother Theo

Dear Theo,

Once again I am in need of funds. I know what a burden I must be to you, but who can I turn to? I need money for materials! I am working almost exclusively with dental floss now, improvising as I go along, and the results are exciting! God! I have not even a penny left for Novocaine! Today I pulled a tooth and had to anesthetize the patient by reading him some Dreiser. Help.

Vincent

Dear Theo,

Will life never treat me decently? I am wracked by despair! My head is pounding! Mrs. Sol Schwimmer is suing me because I made her bridge as I felt it and not to fit her ridiculous mouth! That's right! I can't work to order like a common tradesman! I decided her bridge should be enormous and billowing, with wild, explosive teeth flaring in every direction like fire! Now she is upset because it won't fit in her mouth! She is so bourgeois and stupid, I want to smash her! I tried forcing the false plate in but it sticks out like a star burst chandelier. Still, I find it beautiful. She claims she can't chew! What do I care whether she can chew or not! . . .

Vincent

Dear Theo,

I took some dental X-rays this week that I thought were good. Degas saw them and was critical. He said the composition was bad. All the cavities were bunched in the lower left corner. I explained to him that's how Mrs. Slotkin's mouth looks, but he wouldn't listen. . . .

Vincent

Dear Theo,

Toulouse-Lautrec is the saddest man in the world. He longs more than anything to be a great dentist, and he has real talent, but he's too short to reach his patients' mouths and too proud to stand on anything. Arms over head, he gropes around their lips blindly, and yesterday, instead of putting caps on Mrs. Fitelson's teeth, he capped her chin. Meanwhile, my old friend Monet refuses to work on anything but very, very large

mouths, and Seurat, who is quite moody, has developed a
method of cleaning one tooth at a time until he builds up what
he calls "a full, fresh mouth." It has architectural solidity to
it, but is it dental work? . . .

Vincent

Dear Theo,
Yes, it's true. The ear on sale at Fleishman Brothers' Novelty
Shop is mine. I guess it was a foolish thing to do but I wanted
to send Claire a birthday present last Sunday and everyplace
was closed. Oh, well. Sometimes I wish I had listened to
father and become a painter. It's not exciting but the life is
regular.

Vincent

"If the Impressionists Had Been Dentists"

CHAPTER TWO

An Unsentimental Education

Radio Days

Those Who Can't . . .

Alvy: I remember the staff at our public school. You know, we had a saying that "Those who can't do, teach, and those who can't teach, teach gym." And, of course, those who couldn't do anything, I think, were assigned to our school.

Annie Hall

His Free Play Period

Schoolteacher: Kate and Dennis are doing great! He's integrating beautifully. I'm so pleased. *(To Dennis)* Aren't you?
Alice: Oh.
Schoolteacher: You can really see it in his free play period. Oh, if you want, we can go, uh, talk for a few minutes about a kindergarten that would give him the best chance of eventually getting into an Ivy League school.

Alice

Military School

She was brought up in Darien, Connecticut and, when she was younger, she had a little brother, about six years old. The parents sent the kid to military school. While he was there, he stole jam, or something, and they caught him. They wanted to do things right because it was military school so they held a court martial there. They found the kid guilty. They shot him. They returned to his parents half the tuition.

Monologue

A Rounded Education

Cliff: I promised your father on his deathbed that I would
give you a rounded education, so we probably shouldn't go to
the movies every day. Just once in a while, even though I'd
love to . . . you know? So while we wait for a cab, I'll give you
your lesson for today. Okay? Your lesson is this: Don't listen to
what your schoolteachers tell you. Don't pay attention to that.
Just see what they look like and that's how you know what life
is really going to be like. Okay? You heard it here first.

I think I see a cab. If we run quickly, we can kick the
crutch from that old lady and get it.

Crimes and Misdemeanors

Annie Hall

Radio Days

He Scores Well on an IQ Test

Narrator: Virgil Starkwell attends this school where he scores well on an IQ test although his behavior disturbs the teachers. We interviewed Mrs. Dorothy Lowry, a schoolteacher who remembered Virgil.

Lowry: I remember him clearly. He was the shortest boy in class. And he was very nice but he resisted authority. I remember once he stole a fountain pen. I didn't want to embarrass him so I said to the class, we'll all close our eyes and will the one who took the pen please return it. While our eyes were closed he returned the pen but he took the opportunity to feel all the girls.

Take the Money and Run

Radio Days

Pay More Attention to Your Schoolwork

Mother: Pay more attention to your schoolwork and less to
the radio.

Joe: You always listen to the radio!

Mother: It's different. Our lives are ruined already. You still
have a chance to grow up and be somebody. . . .

Father: You gotta get an education.

Joe: While I'm getting it, can I get the secret compartment
ring?

Mother: We don't have money to waste. . . .

Father: Hey, what do you mean, our lives are already ruined?

Mother: I didn't mean ruined ruined. We're poor, but happy.
But definitely poor.

Radio Days

Playing Ball

For the first fifteen years of my life, I never read. I was just
interested in going out in the street and playing ball. It was
only when I started going out with women who were more cultured and made greater demands on me that I started to feel I
had to keep my end of the conversation up. . . . Even when I
was reading nothing but *Donald Duck* and *Batman* I could
write real prose in school compositions. There was never a
week when the composition I wrote was not the one that was
read to the class.

Newsweek interview

I'm a Philosophy Major

Fielding: Are you a student?
Nancy: Yeah. City College.
Fielding: Oh, it's a great school . . . I ate in their cafeteria once.
Nancy: Oh, really?
Fielding: Yeah, I got trichinosis.
Nancy: Oh! I'm a philosophy major.
Fielding: It's a wonderful thing . . . what is the meaning of life
    and death and why are we here and everything. . . .
Nancy: Right, yeah.
Fielding: Do you like Chinese food?

Bananas

A Great English Student in College

Wendy: I've got to get up at dawn and teach Emily Dickinson
    to a bunch of middle-class crack addicts.
Halley: One of my favorite poets.
Cliff: Me, too.
Halley: "Because I could not stop for death. . . "
Cliff: ". . . he kindly stopped for me." The word "kindly,"
    right?
Lester: "The carriage held but just ourselves and Immortality.
    We slowly drove. He knew no haste. And I had put
    away my Labor and my Leisure, too, for his Civility."
Wendy: Lester was a great English student in college.
Lester: Not that I graduated. I mean, it's amazing: I couldn't
    graduate and this same school now teaches a course
    on existential motifs in my situation comedies.

Crimes and Misdemeanors

College Bulletin

Introduction to Psychology: The theory of human behavior. Why some men are called "lovely individuals" and why there are others you just want to pinch. Is there a split between mind and body, and, if so, which is better to have? . . .

Philosophy I: Everyone from Plato to Camus is read, and the following topics are covered:

Ethics: The categorical imperative, and six ways to make it work for you.

Aesthetics: Is art the mirror of life, or what?

Metaphysics: What happens to the soul after death? How does it manage?

The Absurd: Why existence is often considered silly, particularly for men who wear brown-and-white shoes. Manyness and oneness are studied as they relate to otherness. (Students achieving oneness will move ahead to twoness.)

Rapid Reading: The course will increase reading speed a little each day until the end of the term, by which time the student will be required to read *The Brothers Karamazov* in fifteen minutes. The method is to scan the page and eliminate everything except pronouns from one's field of vision. Soon the pronouns are eliminated. Gradually, the student is encouraged to nap. A frog is dissected. Spring comes. People marry and die. Pinkerton does not return.

"Spring Bulletin"

A History of Hygiene Major

I read an article in *Life* magazine saying there was a sexual revolution going on on college campuses all over the country and I reregistered in New York University to check it out. I used to go there years ago. I was a History of Hygiene major at NYU. And I was thrown out of college and when I was thrown out I got a job. My father had a grocery store on Flatbush Avenue in Brooklyn and he hired me to work for him. I was a delivery boy for my father; it was my first job. I unionized the workers. We struck and drove him out of business. He's always been touchy about it.

Monologue

Woody Allen and Juliette Lewis, *Husbands and Wives.*

A Student at Vassar

"What can I do for you, sugar?"

"I want you to find someone for me."

"Missing person? Have you tried the police?"

"Not exactly, Mr. Lupowitz."

"Call me Kaiser, sugar. All right, so what's the scam?"

"God."

"God?"

"That's right, God. The Creator, the Underlying Principle, the First Cause of Things, the All Encompassing. I want you to find Him for me."

I've had some fruitcakes up in the office before, but when they're built like she was, you listened.

"Why?"

"That's my business, Kaiser. You just find Him."

"I'm sorry, sugar. You got the wrong boy."

"But why?"

"Unless I know all the facts," I said, rising.

"O.K., O.K.," she said, biting her lower lip. She straightened the seam of her stocking, which was strictly for my benefit, but I wasn't buying any at the moment.

"Let's have it on the line, sugar."

"Well, the truth is—I'm not really a nudie model."

"No?"

"No. My name is not Heather Butkiss, either. It's Claire Rosensweig and I'm a student at Vassar. Philosophy major. History of Western Thought and all that. I have a paper due January. On Western religion. All the other kids in the course will hand in speculative papers. But I want to know. Professor Grebanier said if anyone finds out for sure, they're a cinch to pass the course. And my dad's promised me a Mercedes if I get straight A's."

I opened a deck of Luckies and a pack of gum and had one of each. Her story was beginning to interest me. Spoiled coed. High I.Q. and a body I wanted to know better.

"What does God look like?"

"I've never seen Him."

"Well, how do you know He exists?"

"That's for you to find out."

"Oh, great. Then you don't know what He looks like? Or where to begin looking?"

"No. Not really. Although I suspect He's everywhere. In the air, in every flower, in you and me—and in this chair."

"Uh huh." So she was a pantheist. I made a mental note of it and said I'd give her case a try—for a hundred bucks a day, expenses, and a dinner date. She smiled and okayed the deal. We rode down in the elevator together. Outside it was getting dark. Maybe God did exist and maybe He didn't, but somewhere in that city there were sure a lot of guys who were going to try and keep me from finding out.

"Mr. Big"

Deep Philosophical Arguments

Right after the wedding, my wife started turning weird. She went to Hunter College and she got into the philosophy department. She started dressing with black clothes and no makeup and leotards. She pierced her ears one day with a conductor's punch. She used to involve me in deep philosophical arguments and then prove I didn't exist which was infuriating.

Monologue

They Studied Me

Fat Man: Have you studied filmmaking in school?

Sandy: No, no, I didn't study anything in school. They studied me.

Young girl: I understand you studied philosophy at school.

Sandy: Uh, no, that's not true. I did take—I took one course in existential philosophy at New York University, and on the final they gave me ten questions and I couldn't answer a single one of 'em. You know, I left 'em all blank. . . . I got a hundred.

Stardust Memories

CHAPTER THREE

Intellectuals Only Kill Their Own

What Have You Got Against Intellectuals?

Potato-chip Woman: Uh, Mr. Bates, excuse me, what have you got against intellectuals?

Sandy: What? What? Against intellectuals? Nothing. Why?

Potato-chip Woman: Mr. Bates, I've seen all your films. You really feel threatened by them.

Sandy: Threatened? You're kidding. I've always said they're like the Mafia. They only kill their own.

Stardust Memories

Saturn, as seen from the Voyager mission spacecraft, 1981.

The Most Overrated Organ

Mary: Oh, look, there's Saturn. Saturn is the sixth planet from the sun. How many of the satellites of Saturn can you name? There's Mimas—uh, Titan, Dione, Hyperion, of course, uh. . . .

Ike: Nah, I can't name any of them and—and, fortunately, they never come up in conversation.

Mary: Facts. Yeah, I've got a million facts on my fingertips.

Ike: That's right. And they don't mean a thing, right? Because nothing worth knowing can be understood with the mind . . . you know. Everything really valuable has to enter you through a different opening . . . if you'll forgive the disgusting imagery.

Mary: I really don't agree with you. I mean, where would we be without rational thought? Come on.

Ike: No, no, you—you rely too much on your brain. It's a . . . the brain is the most overrated organ, I think.

Woody Allen and Diane Keaton, *Manhattan.*

Manhattan

They Relied Heavily on Logic

Astronomers talk of an inhabited planet named Quelm, so distant from earth that man traveling at the speed of light would take six million years to get there, although they are planning a new express route that will cut two hours off the trip.

Since the temperature on Quelm is thirteen hundred below, bathing is not permitted and the resorts have either closed down or now feature live entertainment.

Because of its remoteness from the center of the solar system, gravity is nonexistent on Quelm and having a large sit-down dinner takes a great deal of planning.

In addition to all these obstacles on Quelm, there is no oxygen to support life as we know it, and what creatures do exist find it hard to earn a living without holding down two jobs.

Legend has it, however, that many billions of years ago the environment was not quite so horrible—or at least no worse than Pittsburgh—and that human life existed. These humans—resembling men in every way except perhaps for a large head of lettuce where the nose normally is—were to a man philosophers. As philosophers they relied heavily on logic and felt that if life existed, somebody must have caused it, and they went looking for a dark-haired man with a tattoo who was wearing a Navy pea jacket.

When nothing materialized, they abandoned philosophy and went into the mail-order business, but postal rates went up and they perished.

"Fabulous Tales and Mythical Beasts"

Tolstoy Is a Full Meal

Gabe: Tolstoy is a full meal. Turgenev, I would say, is a fabulous dessert. That's how I'd characterize him.

Rain: And Doestoevsky?

Gabe: Doestoevsky is a full meal with a vitamin pill and extra wheat germ.

Husbands and Wives

Metterling Was Either a Genius or an Idiot

In 1884, Metterling met Lou Andreas-Salome, and suddenly,
we learn, he required that his laundry be done fresh daily.
Actually, the two were introduced by Nietzsche, who told Lou
that Metterling was either a genius or an idiot and to see if she
could guess which. At that time, the special one-day laundry
service was becoming quite popular on the Continent, particularly with intellectuals, and the innovation was welcomed by
Metterling. For one thing, it was prompt, and Metterling loved
promptness. He was always showing up for appointments early
—sometimes several days early, so that he would have to be
put in a guest room. Lou also loved fresh shipments of laundry
every day. She was like a little child in her joy, often taking
Metterling for walks in the woods and there unwrapping the
latest bundle. She loved undershirts and handkerchiefs, but
most of all she worshipped his shorts. She wrote Nietzsche that
Metterling's shorts were the most sublime thing she had ever
encountered, including *Thus Spake Zarathustra*. Nietzsche
acted like a gentleman about it, but he was always jealous of
Metterling's underwear and told close friends he found it

"Hegelian in the extreme." Lou Salome and Metterling parted company after the Great Treacle Famine of 1886, and while Metterling forgave Lou, she always said of him that "his mind had hospital corners."

"The Metterling Lists"

He Also Refers to Himself as Godard

Obviously, film is a young art and as such is not truly an art but an art within an art employing the devices of mass communication in a linear, non-modal, anti- or non-diversified, creative otherness which we will call density. This concept was first borrowed from the French and then before it could be returned to them, was misplaced by the prop department.

We go to the movies because a picture is playing there. Griffith knew that and said it repeatedly but always to his cat rather than the studio heads. Truffaut, of course, always refers to his films as movies and his movies as films. He also refers to himself as Godard, because Truffaut, he feels, has a pseudo-arty, non-proletarian quality while Godard is much easier to spell.

"Woody, the Would-Be Critic," The New York Times

Jean-Paul Belmondo and Jean Seberg, *Breathless*, 1959.

Leopold Is an Expert on Italian Art

Maxwell: So how did you two meet?

Ariel: We were both tourists at St. Peter's in Rome.

Maxwell *(to Leopold):* You picked her up at the Vatican?

Ariel: My whole life I had heard about the roof of the Sistine Chapel.

Leopold: We met in the basilica, standing before one of the lesser Madonnas. I couldn't resist the impulse to speak with this heavenly creature.

Maxwell: Naturally.

Ariel: Leopold is an expert on Italian art.

Leopold: I had the privilege of escorting Ariel through the Sistine Chapel for the first time in her life and explaining to her exactly why Michelangelo's ceiling is indeed great.

Ariel: When Raphael first laid eyes on it, he fainted.

Maxwell: Had he eaten?

A Midsummer Night's Sex Comedy

Goethe Himself

Finally, and most convincingly, in 1822, Goethe himself notes a strange celestial phenomena. "En route home from the Leipzig Anxiety Festival," he wrote, "I was crossing a meadow, when I chanced to look up and saw several fiery red balls suddenly appear in the southern sky. They descended at a great rate of speed and began chasing me. I screamed that I was a genius and consequently could not run very fast, but my words were wasted. I became enraged and shouted imprecations at them, whereupon they flew away frightened. I related this story to Beethoven, not realizing he had already gone deaf, and he smiled and nodded and said, 'Right.'"

"The UFO Menace"

Dulcy: So that's how a genius seduces a woman.

Leopold: I don't know how Goethe did it but it's the method I use.

A Midsummer Night's Sex Comedy

Kierkegaard Was Right

Last night, I burned all my plays and poetry. Ironically, as I was burning my masterpiece, *Dark Penguin*, the room caught fire, and I am now the object of a lawsuit by some men named Pinchunk and Schlosser. Kierkegaard was right.

"Selections from the Allen Notebooks"

Nancy: Have you ever read the I Ching?
Fielding: Not, not the actual Ching itself but I've dabbled in Kierkegaard.
Nancy: Of course, he's Danish.
Fielding: Yes. He'd be the first to admit that.
Nancy: Yeah, yeah. You know I was just saying to . . . have you ever been to Denmark?
Fielding: Yes. I've been . . . yes, to the Vatican.
Nancy: Oh, to the Vatican. The Vatican's in Rome.
Fielding: Well, it was doing so well in Rome they opened one in Denmark.
Nancy: Oh . . . uh, you know, I was just saying to someone the other day that the Scandinavians seem to have such an instinctive feel for the human condition.
Fielding: That's very wise. You know, that's . . . I think pithy.
Nancy: Oh, well, it was . . . pithy. It had . . . great pith.

Bananas

I Would Most Like to Have Been Socrates

Of all the famous men who ever lived, the one I would most like to have been was Socrates. Not just because he was a great thinker, because I have been known to have some reasonably profound insights myself, although mine invariably revolve around a Swedish airline stewardess and some handcuffs. No, the great appeal for me of this wisest of all Greeks was his courage in the face of death. His decision was not to abandon his principles, but rather to give his life to prove a point. I personally am not quite as fearless about dying and will, after any untoward noise such as a car backfiring, leap directly into the arms of the person I am conversing with. In the end, Socrates's brave death gave his life authentic mean-

Socrates

ing—something my existence lacks totally, although it does possess a minimal relevance to the Internal Revenue Department.

"My Apology"

A Great Student of Socrates

Eamon Bixby: A political fanatic who preached ventriloquism as a cure for the world's ills. He was a great student of Socrates but differed from the Greek philosopher in his idea of the "good life," which Bixby felt was impossible unless everybody weighed the same.

"The Irish Genius"

Einstein Once Wrote Him

Everywhere in Europe Needleman went, students and intellectuals were eager to help him, awed by his reputation. On the run, he found time to publish *Time, Essence, and Reality: A Systematic Reevaluation of Nothingness* and his delightful lighter treatise, *The Best Places to Eat While in Hiding.* Chaim Weizmann and Martin Buber took up a collection and obtained signed petitions to permit Needleman to emigrate to the United States, but at the time the hotel of his choice was full. With German soldiers minutes from his hideout in Prague, Needleman decided to come to America after all, but a scene occurred at the airport when he was overweight with his luggage. Albert Einstein, who was on that same flight, explained to him that if he would just remove the shoe trees from his shoes he could take everything. The two frequently corresponded after that. Einstein once wrote him, "Your work and my work are very similar although I'm still not exactly sure what your work is."

"Remembering Needleman"

Albert Einstein

Prognostication

Finally, we come to Aristonidis, the sixteenth-century count whose predictions continue to dazzle and perplex even the most skeptical. Typical examples are:

"Two nations will go to war, but only one will win." (Experts feel this probably refers to the Russo-Japanese War of 1904–05, an astounding feat of prognostication, considering the fact it was made in 1540.)

"A man in Istanbul will have his hat blocked, and it will be ruined." (In 1850, Abu Hamid, Ottoman warrior, sent his cap out to be cleaned, and it came back with spots.)

"I see a great person, who one day will invent for mankind a garment to be worn over his trousers for protection while cooking. It will be called an 'abron' or 'aprone.'" (Aristonidis meant the apron, of course.)

"A leader will emerge in France. He will be very short and will cause great calamity." (This is a reference either to Napoleon or to Marcel Lumet, an eighteenth-century midget who instigated a plot to rub béarnaise sauce on Voltaire.)

"In the New World, there will be a place named California, and a man named Joseph Cotten will become famous." (No explanation necessary.)

"Examining Psychic Phenomena"

Dysentery

Alvy: I'm so tired of spending evenings making fake insights with people who work for Dysentery.
Robin: Commentary.
Alvy: Oh, really, I heard that Commentary and Dissent had merged and formed Dysentery.

Annie Hall

Joseph Cotten

CHAPTER FOUR

New York vs.
Los Angeles

I Live Here

Alvy: Right, right, so get back to what we were discussing—the failure of the country to get behind New York City is anti-Semitism.

Rob: Max, the city is terribly run.

Alvy: But the—I'm not discussing politics or economics. This is foreskin.

Rob: No, no, no, Max, that's a very convenient out. Every time some group disagrees with you it's because of anti-Semitism.

Alvy: Don't you see? The rest of the country looks upon New York like we're—we're left-wing Communist, Jewish, homosexual, pornographers. I think of us that way, sometimes, and I live here.

Rob: Max, if we lived in California, we could play outdoors every day, in the sun.

Alvy: Sun is bad for you. Everything our parents told us was good is bad. Sun, milk, red meat, college.

Annie Hall

70

This Is Some City

Now he emerged from the hotel and walked up Eighth Avenue.
Two men were mugging an elderly lady. My God, thought
Weinstein, time was when one person could handle that job.
Some city. Chaos everywhere. Kant was right: The mind
imposes order. It also tells you how much to tip. What a won-
derful thing, to be conscious! I wonder what the people in New
Jersey do.

"No Kaddish for Weinstein"

That's New York

Woman: A woman works her whole life on DeKalb Avenue.
I'm reading the *Post*, six hooligans—dope addicts—
grab me and throw me down.
Chorus: There weren't six, there were three.
Woman: Three, six—they had a knife, they wanted my
money.
Diabetes: You should have given it to them.
Woman: I did. They still stabbed me.
Chorus: That's New York. You give'em the money and they
still stab you.
Diabetes: New York? It's everywhere. I was walking with
Socrates in downtown Athens, and two youths from
Sparta jump out from behind the Acropolis and want
all our money.
Woman: What happened?
Diabetes: Socrates proved to them using simple logic that
evil was merely ignorance of the truth.
Woman: And?
Diabetes: They broke his nose.

God (A Play)

Washington Square Park,
New York City.

Crimes and Misdemeanors

My Chronic L.A. Nausea

Rob: We move to L.A. All of show business is out there, Max.

Alvy: No, I cannot. You keep bringing it up, but I don't wanna live in a city where the only cultural advantage is that you can make a right turn on a red light.

Alvy *(in phone booth):* Whatta you mean, where am I? Where do—where do you think I am? I'm out . . . I'm at the Los Angeles Airport. I flew in . . . well, I flew in to see you. . . . Hey, listen, can we not debate this on the telephone because I'm, you know, I feel I got a temperature and I'm getting my chronic Los Angeles nausea. I don't feel so good. . . .

Annie Hall

The Fools in Hollywood

Fritz: They said I was difficult to work with—I went over budget. I spent ten million dollars on a ten-minute short, "Trout Fishing in Quebec." It's still being shown some places, it was a classic. The fools in Hollywood didn't recognize genius. So I spent a fortune on retakes. I couldn't help it! I couldn't get the trout to hold still! Suddenly, I couldn't get into the studios, no one would return my phone calls. Louis B. Mayer said to me, "Gimme your number, I'll call you back." I waited seven years in a phone booth on the corner of Sunset and La Cienega! He never called back!

Take the Money and Run

In Downtown Los Angeles

Someone asked me if I'd tell this story: A long time ago—it's a weird story—I was out in Los Angeles. I was at a party with a very big Hollywood producer. At that time they wanted to make an elaborate CinemaScope musical comedy out of the Dewey Decimal System. They wanted me to work on it and I go out to the producer's building in downtown Los Angeles.

I walk into his elevator and there're no people in the elevator. No buttons on the wall or anything. And I hear a voice say, "Kindly call out your floors, please."

And I look around and I'm alone. I panic. Then I read on the wall that it's a new elevator and it works on a sonic principle. It's all sound, all I have to do is say what floor I want to go to and it takes me there. So I say, "Three, please."

The doors close and the elevator starts going up to three. On the way up, I began to feel very self-conscious because I talk, I think, with a slight New York accent. And the elevator spoke quite well.

I get out. I'm walking out in the hall and I look back. I thought I heard the elevator make a remark. I turn quickly and the doors close and the elevator goes down, you know, and I didn't want to get involved at that time with an elevator in Hollywood, but this is the strange part of the story—that was the normal part.

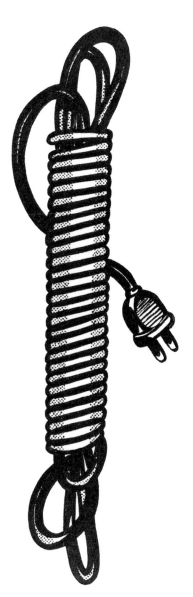

Roy Lichtenstein, *Electric Cord*, 1961.

I have never in my life had good relationships with mechanical objects of any sort. Anything that I can't reason with or kiss or fondle, I get into trouble with. I have a clock that runs counterclockwise for some reason. I have a sunlamp and, as I sit under it, it rains on me. My toaster pops up my toast and shakes it and burns it. I hate my shower. If I'm taking a shower and someone in America uses his water, that's it for me, you know, I leap from the tub, scalded. I have a tape recorder. I paid a hundred and fifty dollars for it and, as I talk into it, it goes, "I know. I know."

About three years ago, I couldn't stand it anymore. I was home one night and I called a meeting of my possessions. I got everything I owned into the living room: my toaster, my clock, my blender. They'd never been in the living room before. And I spoke to them. I was really adorable. I opened with a joke and then I said, "I know what's going on and cut it out."

I spoke to each appliance. I was really articulate. And then I put them back and I felt good.

Two nights later, I'm watching my portable television set and the set begins to jump up and down and I go up to it—I always talk before I hit. I said, "I thought we had discussed this. What's the problem?"

The set kept going up and down. So I hit it and it felt good hitting it. And I beat the hell out of it. I was really great, I tore off the antenna. I felt very virile.

Two days later, I go to my dentist in midtown New York and they have those elevators and I hear a voice say, "Kindly call out your floors, please." I say, "Sixteen." The doors close and the elevator starts going up to sixteen. On the way up, the elevator says to me, "Are you the guy that hit the television set?"

I felt like an ass, you know. And it took me up and down, fast, between floors. It threw me off in the basement and it yelled out something that was anti-Semitic.

And the upshot of the story is, that day, I call my parents. My father was fired. He was technologically unemployed. My father worked for the same firm for twelve years and they fired him. They replaced him with a tiny gadget that does everything my father does—only it does it much better. The depressing thing is—my mother ran out and bought one.

Monologue

Mechanical Incompetence

Playboy: While we're on the subject of your mechanical
    incompetence . . . why do you think machines single
    you out for this kind of treatment?

Allen: There's a definite malevolence in all inanimate
    objects—like the pencil that breaks its point when I
    need it to sign something. It's willing to do that, to
    sacrifice itself, just to impede me. Have you ever
    stepped into a shower and noticed the deliberate
    sequence of ice-cold water, boiling water, ice-cold
    water again? Or the way taxicabs avoid you when you
    need one in a hurry? It's a conscious conspiracy. I
    think I'd like to write a paper on sinks.

Playboy: Sinks?

Allen: There's evil in sinks. They have a decision-making
    ability no one knows about. In short, I have never
    known a noncommitted object. I know this theory of
    mine will erode the very roots of existentialism and
    incur the enmity of French intellectuals, but that's the
    way I feel.

Playboy interview

Great Town, New York

For fifty bucks, I learned, you could "relate without getting
close." For a hundred, a girl would lend you her Bartok
records, have dinner, and then let you watch while she had an
anxiety attack. For one-fifty, you could listen to FM radio with
twins. For three bills, you got the works: A thin Jewish
brunette would pretend to pick you up at the Museum of
Modern Art, let you read her master's, get you involved in a
screaming quarrel at Elaine's over Freud's conception of
women, and then fake a suicide of your choosing—the perfect
evening, for some guys. Nice racket. Great town, New York.

"The Whore of Mensa"

Is the Pope in Town?

Sandy *(talking into car phone):* Yeah. . . . No, I don't think I'm going to make it. We're—we're sitting here in what looks like a truck route or something, you know? I don't know what the hell's going on. . . . You know, it's crazy. The town is jammed. . . . I don't know. Is the Pope in town or some other show-business figure?

Stardust Memories

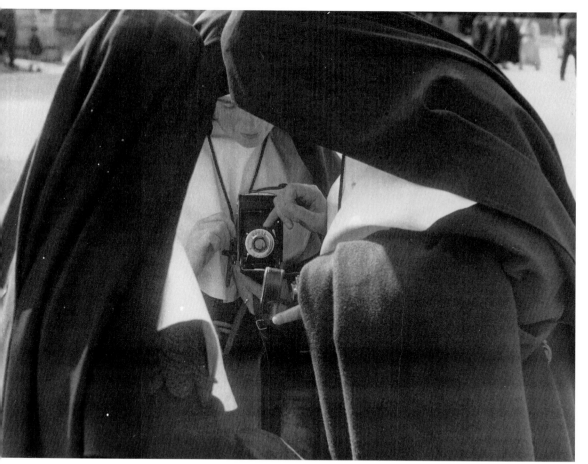

New York City, ca. late 1950s.

Running Down Fifth Avenue

I was watching the "Ed Sullivan Show" one night and Sullivan had on a hypnotist called the Great Renaldo. Renaldo got four guys out of the audience and he hypnotized them. He said to them, "You think you're a fire engine."

I'm home watching. I get drowsy and I fall asleep and I wake up an hour later. I turn the set off and, suddenly, I'm seized with an uncontrollable impulse to dress up in my red flannel underwear, which I do, and I'm looking at myself in the mirror and suddenly the phone rings. I burst out the front door and start running down Fifth Avenue, fast, making a siren noise. At 14th Street, I hit a guy at an intersection who was also wearing red flannel underwear.

We decided to work as one truck.

We start running down to the Village. Suddenly, two guys

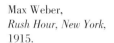

Max Weber,
Rush Hour, New York,
1915.

Ed Sullivan and Woody Allen.

in red flannel underwear pass us, running uptown. We figure
they must know where the fire is. We turn and follow.

At 86th Street, a cop flags us down 'cause there's four
guys in red flannel underwear running up the street and he
says, "You're coming down to headquarters, get into the car."
And I start giggling hysterically 'cause this jerk is trying to get
a fire engine into a lousy little Chevy.

Monologue

Mia Farrow and Woody Allen, *Broadway Danny Rose.*

Can You Picture Danny Rose on a Boat?

Sandy's voice-over: Okay. Now they're gonna go back to Manhattan by boat. A boat, mind you. Can you picture Danny Rose on a boat? I mean, this guy is strictly pavement. He needs the smell of carbon monoxide and litter to feel good. Danny is not meant for water. So naturally, the minute he steps on the boat, he's gone. A lunch he ate in nineteen-fifty-six is beginning to come up on him. He's green, he's dizzy.

Broadway Danny Rose

At Home in the City

I am definitely a child of the city streets, and I feel at home on my own two feet, you know, not in a car or a train or anything like that. In Manhattan, I know the town. I know how to get places. I know where to get cabs. I know where to duck in and go to the bathroom if I have to. And what restaurants to eat at and which ones to avoid. I just feel at home in the city.

Rolling Stone interview

Diane Keaton and Woody Allen, *Manhattan*.

The City He Loved

Ike's voice-over: "Chapter One: He adored New York City.
He idolized it all out of proportion." Uh, no, make that: "He
romanticized it all out of proportion. Now, to him, no matter
what the season was, this was still a town that existed in black
and white and pulsated to the great tunes of George
Gershwin." Ah, now let me start this over.

"Chapter One: He was too romantic about Manhattan as
he was about everything else. He thrived on the hustle-bustle
of the crowds and the traffic.

"To him, New York meant beautiful women and street-
smart guys who seemed to know all the angles." Nah, no . . .
corny, too corny for my taste. I mean, let me try to be more
profound. . . .

"Chapter One: He was as tough and romantic as the city
he loved. Behind his black-rimmed glasses was the coiled sexual power of a jungle cat." I love this. "New York was his
town. And it always would be."

Manhattan

CHAPTER FIVE

Love: The Good Sentimental

A Most Complex Emotion

Dr. Yang: Love. Love is—most complex emotion. Human beings—unpredictable. No logic to emotions. Where there is no logic, there is no rational thought. Where there's no rational thought, there can be much romance but much suffering.

Alice

For all my education, accomplishments and so-called wisdom, I can't fathom my own heart.
Hannah and Her Sisters

Should I marry W.? Not if she won't tell me the other letters in her name.
"Selections from the Allen Notebooks"

A Very Strange Paradox

Professor Levy: You will notice that what we are aiming at when we fall in love is a very strange paradox. The paradox consists of the fact that when we fall in love we are seeking to re-find all or some of the people to whom we were attached as children. On the other hand, we ask our beloved to correct all of the wrongs that these early parents or siblings inflicted upon us. So that love contains in it the contradiction. The attempt to return to the past and the attempt to undo the past.

Crimes and Misdemeanors

On Love

Is it better to be the lover or the loved one? Neither, if your cholesterol is over six hundred. By love, of course, I refer to romantic love—the love between man and woman, rather than between mother and child, or a boy and his dog, or two head-waiters.

The marvelous thing is that when one is in love there is an impulse to sing. This must be resisted at all costs, and care must be taken to see that the ardent male doesn't "talk" the lyrics of songs. To be loved, certainly, is different from being admired, as one can be admired from afar but to really love someone it is essential to be in the same room with the person, crouching behind the drapes.

To be a really good lover, then, one must be strong and yet tender. How strong? I suppose being able to lift fifty pounds should do it. Bear in mind also that to the lover the loved one is always the most beautiful thing imaginable, even though to a stranger she may be indistinguishable from an order of smelts. Should the beholder have poor eyesight, he can ask the nearest person which girls look good. (Actually, the prettiest ones are almost always the most boring, and that is why some people feel there is no God.)

"The joys of love are but a moment long," sang the trouba-dour, "but the pain of love endures forever." This was almost a hit song, but the melody was too close to "Yankee Doodle Dandy."

"The Early Essays"

The Perfect Woman

Sandy: But you know, I've never been able to fall in love. I've never been able to find the perfect woman. There's always something wrong. And then I met Doris. A wonderful woman. Great personality. But for some reason, I'm just not turned on sexually by her. Don't ask me why. And then I met Rita. An animal. Nasty, mean, trouble. And I love going to bed with her. Though afterward I always wished that I was back with Doris. And then, I thought to myself, if only I could put Doris's brain in Rita's body. Wouldn't that be wonderful? And I thought, Why not? What the hell, I'm a surgeon.

Tony: Surgeon? Where'd you study medicine, in Transylvania?

Sandy: So, I performed the operation and everything went perfectly. I switched their personalities and I took all the badness and put it over there. And I made Rita into a warm, wonderful, charming, sexy, sweet, giving, mature woman. And then I fell in love with Doris.

Blind Man: Do you really feel there's such a thing as a perfect mate? I mean, don't you think the basis of any mature relationship is really compromise?

Sandy: I think any relationship, uh, is not based on either compromise or maturity or perfection or any of that. It's really based on luck. You, you know that's the key thing. People don't like to acknowledge that because it means a loss of control, but you really have to be lucky.

Stardust Memories

Undoubtedly, dear reader, you have heard the expression, "a body that wouldn't quit." Well, Tiffany's body would not only not quit, it wouldn't take five minutes off for a coffee break.

"The Lunatic's Tale"

Gena Rowlands and Gene
Hackman, *Another Woman.*

I Knew I Was in Love

I knew I was in love. First of all, I was nauseous. You know, I
never met such a pretty girl and I guess I'm sensitive because
real beauty makes me want to gag.

I don't know how to act with girls. You know, I'm shy. I'm
just nervous around women, I have a tendency to dribble. The
only girl I'd known was a girl in the neighborhood who was not
an attractive girl. I used to make obscene phone calls to her,
collect. She used to accept the charges all the time but nothing
ever happened.

And here I'm lying through my teeth. I mean, I can't tell
Louise that I was in jail and that I rob and steal and never did
an honest day's work in my life 'cause, you know, some people
hold these things against you.

But she was so sweet and we just walked in the park and I

Woody Allen and Mia Farrow,
Hannah and Her Sisters.

was so touched by her that, after fifteen minutes, I wanted to
marry her and, after half an hour, I completely gave up the
idea of snatching her purse.

I wanted to tell her I wasn't with the Philharmonic but she
was so impressed by it. And when she asked me some questions about Mozart, she got suspicious because for a moment I
couldn't place the name.

I don't know, when it comes to women. In prison, I
remember the psychiatrist asked me if I had a girl and I said,
"no." He asked me, well, did I think that sex was dirty and I
said: "It is if you do it right."

All I know is my heart was really pounding and I felt a
funny tingling all over—I don't know, I was either in love or I
had smallpox.

Take the Money and Run

If I Didn't Love Deeply

Sonja: But I tell you I feel as though my life would be wasted
if I didn't love deeply with the man whose mind I
respected, whose spirituality equaled mine, and who
had the same . . . oh, lustful appetite for sensual pas-
sion that drives me insane!

Boris: You're an incredibly complex woman.

Sonja: I guess you could say I'm half-saint, half-whore.

Boris: Here's hoping I get the half that eats.

Love and Death

Stardust Memories

The Perfect Guy for You

Rita: I know the perfect guy for you.

Babs: Who?

Rita: He's brilliant. He's attractive.

Babs: Well, who is it? What? There's a hitch. I'm waiting.

Rita: He's in prison.

Babs: Rita, I would say that's a drawback.

Rita: Nothing terrible. Insider trading. He made a fortune in the market and he'll be out soon. Very soon. A couple of years.

Babs: You mean with good behavior?

Crimes and Misdemeanors

Charlotte Rampling and Woody Allen, *Stardust Memories.*

Kamikaze Women

Gabe: There are a number of very, very good professors who are notorious for seducing their female pupils. This goes on because it's a cinch. You know, they look up to them and they're older men and their students are flattered by the attention. It's something I've never done. I don't say I haven't had daydreams in class at times. Some of these women are very attractive and interesting. But I've never acted on it. I've never cheated on Judy or any other relationship in my life. That has not been my style. But once, many years ago, one time I was living with this fabulous, interesting woman . . . Harriet Harmon.

I'm ashamed to say this but Harriet Harmon remains the great love of my life. It was very passionate. I loved her intensely. We just made love everywhere. She was sexually carnivorous. We did it in stalled elevators and in bushes and people's houses. At parties in the bathroom and, I hate to say, in the back of cars—she'd put a coat on our laps and then, suddenly grab my hand and stick it between her legs. I mean, she was really something. She was highly libidinous. You know what I mean?

She wanted to make love to other women. She got into dope. She would break that thing you sniff when she'd have her orgasm. And, you know, for me, I was getting a real education. I was fascinated. I was just absolutely nuts about her.

She wound up in an institution. It's not funny. It's very sad. She was great, but nuts.

I've always had this penchant for what I call "kamikaze women." I call them kamikaze because they, you know, they crash their plane. They're self-destructive. But they crash it into you and you die along with them.

As soon as there's a challenge, very little chance of it working out, or no chance, or there's going to be tremendous obstacles, something clicks in my mind. Maybe that's because I'm a writer. But some dramatic or aesthetic component becomes right and I go after that person. There's a certain dramatic ambiance. I fall in love with the person, with the situation. Of course, it has not worked out well for me.

Husbands and Wives

Woody Allen and Mariel Hemingway, *Manhattan*.

God's Answer to Job

Tracy: Quit fighting it. You know you're crazy about me.
Ike: I am. You—you—you're . . . look, you're God's answer
        to Job, you know? You would've ended all—all argu-
        ment between them. I mean, He would've pointed to
        you and said, "I do a lot of terrible things, but I can
        also make one of these." And then—then Job
        would've said, "Eh, okay—well, you win."

Manhattan

Laws and Proverbs

The lion and the calf shall lie down together but the calf won't
get much sleep.

The wicked at heart probably know something.

Whosoever loveth wisdom is righteous but he that keepeth
company with fowl is weird.

"The Scrolls"

Adultery, Alice

Alice: I met a man who reminds me of you. . . . He's like you, he's irresponsible and temperamental—but he's cute, you know.

Eddie: Thou shalt not commit adultery, Alice. That's not my line, I read it.

Alice

God, She's Beautiful

Eliot's voice-over: God, she's beautiful. She's got the prettiest eyes, and she looks so sexy in that sweater . . . I just want to be alone with her and kiss her and tell her how much I love her and take care of her. Stop it, you idiot. She's your wife's sister. But I can't help it. I'm consumed by her. It's been months now. I dream about her. I, I think about her at the office. Oh, Lee. What am I going to do? I hear myself mooning over you and it's disgusting. Before, when she squeezed past me in the doorway, and I smelled that perfume on the back of her neck, Jesus, I, I thought I was gonna swoon! Easy . . . you're a dignified financial advisor. It doesn't look good for you to swoon.

Hannah and Her Sisters

Barbara Hershey, *Hannah and Her Sisters*.

It's Better for Your Heart

Cliff: See, this is what I need. A little interest in my work. A little encouragement or something. May I ask you something? I got a bottle of champagne as a prize. It was sent to me from Paris. I got an honorable mention, you know, for a little documentary I did on leukemia. And, um, you want some champagne?

Halley: I never say no to champage. Or caviar.

Cliff: Okay, that's perfect. I have no caviar, of course. I have oat bran. It's better for your heart.

Crimes and Misdemeanors

Mickey: The heart is a very, very resilient little muscle.

Hannah and Her Sisters

Sure, He's Fictional

Cecilia: I just met a wonderful new man. Sure, he's fictional but you can't have everything.

The Purple Rose of Cairo

Mia Farrow and Jeff Daniels, *The Purple Rose of Cairo.*

Grant Wood, *American Gothic*, 1930. Scott and Zelda Fitzgerald, May, 1923.

Something Real

There was something real about the Fitzgeralds; their values were basic. They were such modest people, and when Grant Wood later convinced them to pose for his *American Gothic* I remember how flattered they were. All through their sittings, Zelda told me, Scott kept dropping the pitchfork.

I became increasingly friendly with Scott in the next few years, and most of our friends believed that he based the protagonist of his latest novel on me and that I had based my life on his previous novel and I finally wound up getting sued by a fictional character.

"A Twenties Memory"

Is Sex Real?

Actor: You idiot, you're fictional, she's Jewish—you know what the children will be like?...

Doris: Is sex real?

Writer: Even if it's not, it's still one of the best fake activities a person can do. *(He grabs her, she pulls back.)*

Doris: Don't. Not here.

Writer: Why not?

Doris: I don't know. That's my line.

Writer: Have you ever made it with a fictional character?

Doris: The closest I ever came was an Italian.

God (A Play)

Something Seductive About Me

I played Las Vegas for the first time. Let's see, I'm not a gambler, you should know that about me, too. I went to the racetrack once in my life and I bet on a horse called Battlegun and all the horses come out and mine is the only horse in the race with training wheels.

You have to believe me when I tell you this . . . there is something seductive about me when I shoot crap. And I'm at the crap table and I'm dicing and a very provocative woman comes up to me and she begins to size me up. And I take her upstairs to my hotel room. I shut the door, remove my glasses, show her no mercy. I unbutton my shirt and she unbuttons her shirt. I smile, she smiles. I remove my shirt, she removes her shirt and I wink and she winks. I remove my pants and she removes her pants and I realize I'm looking into a mirror.

I don't want to go into details but I was pulling glass out of my legs for two weeks.

Monologue

They Threw Me Out of Masters and Johnson

Doctor: I'm Dr. Bernardo. You must be Jeff and Miss Lacey. . . .

Jeff: I hope to be of great help in these sexual experiments, Doctor.

Helen: I think it's wonderful how you men of science have finally gotten around to sex. All the girls at the paper were so thrilled with your work on respiration during orgasm.

Doctor: A mere trifle compared to my real work.

Jeff: I read recently you stated that the length of the average penis should be nineteen inches. Isn't that a little long, Doctor?

Doctor: Does it sound mad? That's what they called me at Masters and Johnson Clinic. Mad. Because I had visions of exploring sexual areas undreamed of by lesser human beings. It was I who first discovered how to make a man impotent by hiding his hat. I was the first one to explain the connection between excessive masturbation and entering politics. It was I who first said that clitoral orgasms should not be only for women. They laughed at me . . . ridiculed me . . . called me mad, but I showed them. They threw me out of Masters and Johnson . . . no severance pay. . . .

Everything You Always Wanted
to Know About Sex . . .

Sex with You

Reporter: Oh, sex with you is really a Kafkaesque experience.

Alvy: Oh, tsch, thank you. H'm.

Reporter: I mean that as a compliment.

Alvy: I think—I think there's too much burden placed on the orgasm, you know, to make up for empty areas of life.

Reporter: Who said that?

Alvy: Uh, oh, I don't know. It might have been Leopold and Loeb.

Annie Hall

Sex and Love

Ariel: Tell me something, if you lusted after me so, why
weren't you in love with me? Can the two feelings be
so separate?
Andrew: Sometimes I think the two are totally different. Sex
alleviates tension and love causes it.

A Midsummer Night's Sex Comedy

It's very hard to get your head and heart to work together in
life. In my case, they're not even friendly.

Crimes and Misdemeanors

He knew there was a difference between sex and love, but felt
that either act was wonderful unless one of the partners happened to be wearing a lobster bib. Women, he reflected, were a
soft, enveloping presence. Existence was a soft, enveloping
presence, too. Sometimes, it enveloped you totally. Then you
could never get out again except for something really important, like your mother's birthday or jury duty. Cloquet often
thought there was a great difference between Being and Being-
in-the-World, and figured that no matter which group he
belonged to, the other was definitely having more fun.

"The Condemned"

Sex Without Love

Boris: I know what's bothering you, you're worried whether
you're gonna be a stimulating enough wife for me.
Whether it's possible to live up to the chores and
obligations of married life. But, it's gonna be a cinch,
I promise. I have no bad habits, at all. Granted, I have
a few eccentricities. I won't eat any food that begins
with the letter "F." Like chicken, for instance.
That's—
Sonja: Boris, I don't love you. . . . I mean, I love you, but, I'm
not in love with you.

Boris: Sonja, do you even know what love means?

Sonja: There are so many different kinds of love, Boris. There's love between a man and a woman, love between a mother and a son.

Boris: Two women. Let's not forget my favorite.

Sonja: But then, there's the love I've always dreamed of ever since I was a little girl.

Boris: Yeah?

Sonja: The love between two extraordinary individuals.

Boris: Sonja . . . .

Sonja: Oh, don't Boris! Please! Sex without love is an empty experience.

Boris: Yes, but—as empty experiences go—it's one of the best!

Love and Death

How Can I Compete?

Cliff: I'm completely in love with Halley and Lester is starting to make his move. I can see it. And he wants her just for conquest, I can tell. You know, it's so shallow, and I'm crazy about her. How can I compete with the guy because he's rich and famous. He's successful.

Jenny: Oh come on. He's no competition for you.

Cliff: Oh, God bless you for saying that, sweetheart, really. But you'll find as you go through life that great depth and smoldering sensuality does not always win. I'm sorry to say.

Crimes and Misdemeanors

I Dated Her Once

Allen (on phone): Hello, is this the Perry residence? Ummm, can I speak to Marilyn? Umm, Allan Felix, an old friend of hers from Midwood High School. I dated her once.

Do you remember? I'm stunned, it was eleven years ago. That's right. Right. Short, with red hair and glasses. Yes. No, no, no, that's cleared up.

Well . . . how can I get in touch with your daughter? Oh

really? She still feels that way? Well, it's been eleven years. When did you last speak to her? Yeah? Last week? And she specified that she didn't want you to give me the number? I see. Okay, thank you. Yes. Okay.

Play It Again, Sam

A Relentless Spate of Blind Dates

Well-meaning friends fixed me up with a relentless spate of blind dates, all unerringly from the pages of H. G. Lovecraft. Ads, answered out of desperation, in the *New York Review of Books*, proved equally futile, as the "thirtyish poetess" was sixtyish, the "coed who enjoys Bach and Beowulf" looked like Grendel, and the "Bay Area bisexual" told me I didn't quite coincide with either of her desires. This is not to imply that now and again an apparent plum would not somehow emerge: a beautiful woman, sensual and wise with impressive credentials and winning ways. But, obeying some age-old law, perhaps from the Old Testament or Egyptian Book of the Dead, she would reject me. And so it was that I was the most miserable of men.

"The Lunatic's Tale"

A Bad History with Blind Dates

Now, when I went back to school, suddenly, everybody wanted to fix me up with women. And I have had a very bad history with blind dates. You must not misunderstand me. I believe that sex is a beautiful thing between two people—between five it's fantastic.

Monologue

Do You Want to Perform Sex with Me?

Luna: Do you want to perform sex with me?
Miles: Perform sex? I don't think I'm up to a performance, but I'll rehearse with you, if you like.

Sleeper

101

I've Never Paid for Sex

Dorry: I know what's on your mind. Let's go up to the bedroom.

Kleinman: I've never paid for sex.

Dorry: You just think you haven't.

Shadows and Fog

There Goes Another Novel

Annie: M'm, that was so nice. That was nice.

Alvy: As Balzac said, "There goes another novel." Jesus, you were great.

Annie: Oh, yeah?

Alvy: Yeah.

Annie: Yeah?

Alvy: Yeah, I'm—I'm a wreck. . . . Really, I mean it. I'll never play the piano again.

Annie: You're really nuts. I don't know, you really thought it was good? Tell me.

Alvy: Good? I was—

Annie: No.

Alvy: No, that was the most fun I've ever had without laughing.

Annie Hall

You Were Fantastic Last Night in Bed

Allen: You were fantastic last night in bed.

Linda: Oh, thanks.

Allen: How do you feel now?

Linda: I think the Pepto Bismol helped.

Play It Again, Sam

Woody Allen and Diane Keaton, *Annie Hall*.

That Was Like a Religious Experience

Andrew: I'm still spinning, Adrian. That was like a religious
experience.

Adrian: It's only the beginning. Wait till everybody's gone and
we're alone. I'll show you what Dulcy calls a Mexican
Cartwheel.

Andrew: I'm in shock . . . my sinuses have been cleared forever.

Adrian: Can you forgive me?

Andrew: Forgive you? I'd be happy to ordain you.

Adrian: And Maxwell, too?

Andrew: I forgive everyone everything tonight—I feel I can
heal people.

A Midsummer Night's Sex Comedy

In an Elevator

Renee: Who'd have thought? In an elevator!
Michael: It's the safest place in the world providing the combined weight of the two people doesn't exceed 1,400 pounds.

What's New Pussycat?

She Was Violated

I got married for the second time. I should've known something was wrong with my first wife when I brought her home to meet my parents—they approved of her but my dog died.

I got to be careful about what I say about her publicly because she's suing me. I don't know whether you read about that in the paper or not but I'm getting sued because I made a nasty remark about her, she didn't like that. She lives on the Upper West Side of Manhattan and she was coming home late at night and she was violated. That's how they put it in the New York paper, "She was violated." They asked me to comment on it. I said, "Knowing my ex-wife, it probably was not a moving violation."

Monologue

Nothing Sexier

Alice: These past few weeks have been really fun for me.
Joe: You were so relaxed this morning when we were back in my place. . . . Very uninhibited. . . . Nothing sexier than a lapsed Catholic.

Alice

Olive Chomsky found herself delightfully free from the curse of being a sex object. As Darwin taught us, she soon developed a keen intelligence, and while not perhaps the equal of Hannah Arendt's, it did permit her to recognize the follies of astrology and marry.

"The Lunatic's Tale"

The Good Sentimental

Sandy: No, you're wrong! I'm telling you, I was, I was thinking about a lot of unusual things over the weekend and I feel much . . . I feel much lighter. Do you know what I mean? And, and, um, I had a very, very remarkable idea for a new ending for my movie, you know? We're, we're on a train and there are, there are many sad people on it, you know? And, and I have no idea where it's heading . . . could be anywhere, could be the same junkyard. And, uh, but it's not as terrible as I originally thought it was because . . . because, you know, we like each other, and, uh, you know, we have some laughs, and there's a lot of closeness, and the whole thing is a lot easier to take.

Isobel: I don't like it. . . . It's too sentimental.

Sandy: So? But so what? It's the good sentimental. That's what you—but there's this character that's based on you that's, that's very warm and very giving and you're absolutely, um, nuts over me. You're just crazy about me. You think I'm the most wonderful thing in the world, and you're in love with me, and you're. . . . And, and despite the fact that I do a lot of foolish things, 'cause you realize that deep down I'm not evil or anything, you know? Just sort of floundering around. Just, just ridiculous, maybe. You know, just searching, okay?

Isobel: I don't think it's realistic.

Sandy: What? Now? This is . . . now you're gonna bring up realism, after . . . after? This is a hell of a time to . . . now, I know one thing: that a, that a huge big wet kiss would go a long way to selling this idea. I'm very serious. I think, I think this is a big, big finish. Do you know what I mean?

Stardust Memories

Marion: I often wonder about real love, or I should say, I keep myself from thinking about it. I don't mean the kind I've experienced but something much, much deeper, much more intense. But then I become frightened because I feel too much.

Another Woman

Woody Allen and Diane Keaton, *Annie Hall.*

I Lerve You

Alvy: You are extremely sexy.

Annie: No, I'm not.

Alvy: Unbelievably sexy. Yes, you are. Because . . . you know what you are? You're, you're polymorphously perverse.

Annie: Well, what does—what does that mean? I don't know what that is.

Alvy: Uh . . . uh, you're, you're exceptional in bed because you got—you get pleasure in every part of your body when I touch you. . . . You know what I mean? Like the tip of your nose, and if I stroke your teeth or your kneecaps, you get excited.

Annie: Come on. Yeah. You know what? You know, I like you, I really mean it. I really do like you.

Alvy: Do you love me?

Annie: Do I love you?

Alvy: That's the key question.

Annie: Yeah.

Alvy: I know you've only known me a short while.

Annie: Well, I certainly, I think that's very—yeah, yeah
yeah. Do you love me?

Alvy: I, uh, love is, too weak for what—

Annie: Yeah.

Alvy: I . . . I lerve you. You know, I lo-ove you. I-I luff you.
There are two "f's." I have to invent—of course, I love
you.

Annie Hall

Pigeons, Penguins and Catholics

Ike: Well, I'm old-fashioned. I don't believe in extramarital
relationships. I think people should mate for life, like
pigeons or Catholics.

Manhattan

Dr. Yang: Tell me what you see.

Alice: Penguins.

Dr. Yang: What about penguins?

Alice: They mate for life.

Dr. Yang: Yes. You think penguins are Catholics?

Alice

Radio Days

We're Together Forever

Ceil: Why don't you take me to the Copacabana or El Morocco?

Abe: Take the gas pipe.

Ceil: You'd have been happier married to Rita Hayworth?

Abe: You have to ask?

Ceil: Those show business types get divorced every six weeks. But we're together forever.

Abe: I may take the gas pipe.

Radio Days

Oh, Please, Say It in French

Fielding: I love you. I love you.

Nancy: Oh, say it in French. Oh, please, say it in French.

Fielding: I don't know French.

Nancy: Oh, please . . . please!

Fielding: How about Hebrew?

Bananas

A Meaningful Relationship

Did anyone I know ever have a "meaningful relationship"? My parents stayed together forty years, but that was out of spite. Greenglass, another doctor at the hospital, married a woman who looked like a Feta cheese "because she's kind." Iris Merman cheated with any man who was registered to vote in the tri-state area. Nobody's relationship could actually be called happy.

"The Lunatic's Tale"

Life is truly chaos, I thought. Feelings are so unpredictable. How does anyone ever stay married for forty years? This, it seems, is more of a miracle than the parting of the Red Sea, though my father, in his naïveté, holds the latter to be a greater achievement.

"Retribution"

Luna: But Miles, don't you see, meaningful relationships between men and women don't last. That was proven by science. You see, there's a chemical in our bodies that makes it so that we all get on each other's nerves sooner or later.

Miles: Hey, that's science, I don't believe in science. You know, science is an intellectual dead end. It's a lot of little guys with tweed suits, cutting up frogs, and, and, foundation grants and . . .

Luna: Oh, I see, you don't believe in science, and you also don't believe that the political systems work and you don't believe in God, huh? So then, what do you believe in?

Miles: Sex and death. Two things that come once in my life-time. But at least after death you're not nauseous.

Sleeper

Laura: You think at your age you could meet someone and fall in love?

Marion's Father: One hopes at my age to build up an immunity.

Another Woman

109

Paul Klee,
Handbill for Comedians,
1938.

My One Love Letter

Halley: I wanted to give you this love letter back.
Clifford: It's my one love letter.
Halley: It's beautiful. I'm just the wrong person.
Clifford: It's just as well. I plagiarized most of it from James
Joyce. You probably wondered why all the references
to Dublin.

Crimes and Misdemeanors

I'm Not Leader Enough for Her

Fielding: Can you believe that? She says I'm not leader
enough for her. Who's she looking for, Hitler?

Paul: Women are very tempermental.

Fielding: We went everyplace together. We did everything.
We fell in love. I fell in love. She just stood there.

Paul: Did you have trouble with her in bed?

Fielding: Are you kidding? Do I look like the kind of guy that
would have trouble in bed? I didn't, I didn't. . . . I'm
so depressed! I'd kill myself if I thought that she
would marry me!

Paul: Well, what are you going to do?

Fielding: I gotta get out of here! I'm going down to San
Marcos. We were going to go down there together on a
trip. We were going to write a paper on it. She was
going to write it. I was going to type it.

Bananas

To Love Is to Suffer

Natasha: It's a very complicated situation, cousin Sonja. I'm
in love with Alexi. He loves Alicia. . . . Alicia's having
an affair with Lev. Lev loves Tatiana. Tatiana loves
Simkin. Simkin loves me. I love Simkin, but in a
different way than Alexi. Alexi loves Tatiana like a
sister. Tatiana's sister loves Trigorian like a brother.
Trigorian's brother is having an affair with my sister
whom he likes physically, but not spiritually.

Sonja: Natasha . . . it's getting a little late.

Natasha: The firm of Mishkin and Mishkin is sleeping with
the firm of Taskov and Taskov.

Sonja: Natasha, to love is to suffer. To avoid suffering, one
must not love. But, then one suffers from not loving.
Therefore, to love is to suffer, not to love is to suffer, to
suffer is to suffer. To be happy is to love, to be happy
then, is to suffer, but, suffering makes one unhappy,
therefore, to be unhappy one must love, or love to suffer, or suffer from too much happiness, I hope you're
getting this down.

Natasha: I never want to marry. I just want to get divorced.

Love and Death

Love Fades

Alvy: That's fine. That's fine. That's great! Well, I don't know what I did wrong. I mean, I can't believe this. Somewhere she cooled off to me! Is it—is it something I did?

Woman on the street: Never something you do. That's how people are. Love fades.

Annie Hall

A Dead Shark

Annie: Alvy, uh, let's face it. You know some—I don't think our relationship is working.

Alvy: I know. A relationship, I think, is like a shark, you know? It has to constantly move forward or it dies. And I think what we got on our hands is a dead shark.

Annie Hall

Unrequited Love

Jenny: Let me tell you something. Men and women want very
different things out of sex. They've never forgiven
each other.

Irmy: Where would you say love came in?

Dorry: Oh, now there's only one kind of love that lasts. That's
unrequited love. It stays with you forever.

Shadows and Fog

Marrying for Love Is a Very Recent Idea

Bea: You think I'm too demanding.

Mother: I do. I think you have these qualities that you
demand, and when you meet a nice man you disqual-
ify him for the smallest fault.

Bea: That's not true.

Mother: So what was wrong with Nat Bernstein?

Bea: He wore white socks with a tuxedo.

Mother: That's not a good enough reason, and then when you
fall in love with somebody there is always something
wrong with him.

Bea: They all *seem* fine.

Mother: I don't know. You got this sixth sense for picking
losers. Sometimes I wonder, do you really want to get
married?

Bea: More than anything. Don't you think I want to have a
child before it's too late? God, how I envy you. I just
want it to be perfect.

Mother: Well, it's never perfect. I mean, if you wait for perfect, you don't get pregnant. You wind up with your
teeth in a glass of water.

Bea: Easy for you to say.

Mother: I compromised when I picked Martin. I mean, I
wanted someone tall and handsome and rich. Three
out of three I gave up.

Bea: Oh, I think you did right to compromise.

Mother: Why? You don't think I could have done better than
Martin?

Bea: I know. You could have married Sam Slotkin. So why
didn't you?

Michael Tucker, *Radio Days*.

Mother: Sam Slotkin was a mortician. He always smelled of
formaldehyde.

Bea: Ugh.

Mother: And don't think Martin didn't compromise when he
picked me. I mean, he always dreamed of being a
business tycoon, having a beautiful blonde wife. I tell
him the day he becomes a tycoon, I'll dye my hair.

Bea: Well, at least you have each other. That's all I want,
someone.

Mother: So you have to lower your standards a little. You
know, marrying for love is a very recent idea. In the
old country, they didn't marry for love. A man married
a woman because he needed an extra mule.

Bea: It's you who listens to the romantic radio soap operas.

Mother: I like to daydream. But I have my two feet planted
firmly on my husband.

Radio Days

How I Feel About Relationships

Alvy's voice-over: I thought of that old joke, you know, this guy goes to a psychiatrist and says, "Doc, my brother's crazy. He thinks he's a chicken." And, the doctor says, "Why don't you turn him in?" And the guy says, "I would, but I need the eggs." Well, I guess that's pretty much how I feel about relationships. You know, they're totally irrational and crazy and absurd and . . . but, I guess we keep going through it because, uh, most of us need the eggs.

Annie Hall

When It Comes to Sex

The truth is I've learned one thing from this whole situation and that is when it comes to sex there are certain things that should always be left unknown and, with my luck, they probably will be.

Everything You Always
Wanted to Know About Sex . . .

Something I Was Not Getting in My Marriage

Gabe: How could I be, you know, a hundred percent honest with Judy? I felt that I loved her but what was I going to say? That I'm becoming infatuated with a twenty-year-old girl? That I'm sleepwalking into a mess and I've learned nothing over the years?

Interviewer: Then why didn't you stop yourself?

Gabe: I craved something I was not getting in my marriage and Rain—you know, there was a certain excitement there for me.

Interviewer: Rain had a boyfriend.

Gabe: I know. Everything about it was wrong. But that did not deter me. That, if anything, made me, as usual— you know, there was something interesting.

Interviewer: So you have a self-destructive streak?

Gabe: I don't know. My heart does not know from logic.

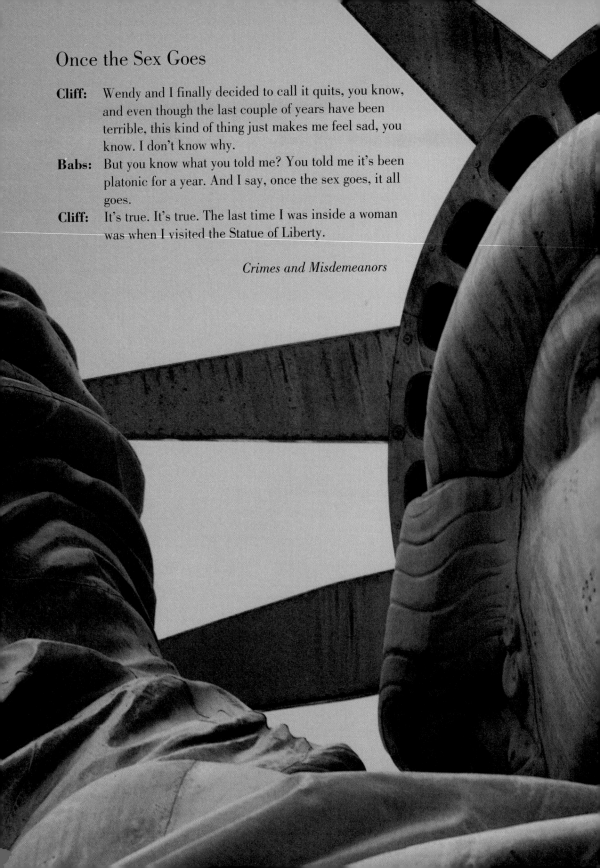

Once the Sex Goes

Cliff: Wendy and I finally decided to call it quits, you know, and even though the last couple of years have been terrible, this kind of thing just makes me feel sad, you know. I don't know why.

Babs: But you know what you told me? You told me it's been platonic for a year. And I say, once the sex goes, it all goes.

Cliff: It's true. It's true. The last time I was inside a woman was when I visited the Statue of Liberty.

Crimes and Misdemeanors

I Had a Rough Marriage

I wanted to discuss my marriage or, as it was known, The Oxbow Incident. I had a rough marriage. Well, my wife was an immature woman and, that's all I can say. See if this isn't immature to you: I would be home in the bathroom, taking a bath, and my wife would walk in whenever she felt like and sink my boats.

It was partially my fault that we got a divorce. I had a lousy attitude toward her. For the first year of marriage, I tended to place my wife underneath a pedestal.

We used to argue and fight and finally we decided we should either take a vacation or get a divorce. We discussed it very maturely and we decided on the divorce because we felt we had a limited amount of money to spend. A vacation in Bermuda is over in two weeks but a divorce is something that you always have.

I saw myself free again, living in the Village in a bachelor apartment with a wood-burning fireplace, a shaggy rug and, on the walls, one of those Picassos by Van Gogh. Great swinging airline hostesses running amok in the apartment. I got very excited and I laid it right on the line with her. I came right to the point. I said, "Quasimodo, I want a divorce."

And she said, "Great, get the divorce."

But it turns out in New York State they have a strange law that says you can't get a divorce unless you can prove adultery. That is weird because the Ten Commandments say, "Thou shalt not commit adultery," but New York state says you have to.

For awhile there, it's like a toss-up between God and Rockefeller.

So I figured one of us has got to commit adultery to get the divorce. I volunteered.

But when you're married and out of circulation there's not that many women who you can have a thing with. The only woman I knew was my wife's best friend, Nancy. So I called up Nancy on the phone and I asked her if she would have adultery with me. She said, "Not even if it would help the Space Program." Which I took as a negative at the time.

What finally happened was my wife committed adultery for me. She's always been more mechanically inclined than I was.

Monologue

Marc Chagall, *Double Portrait with Wine Glass*, 1917-18.

Empty Dreams Are North

Weinstein rang the bell to Harriet's apartment, and suddenly she was standing before him. Swelling to maculate giraffe, as usual, thought Weinstein. It was a private joke that neither of them understood.

"Hello, Harriet," he said.

"Oh, Ike," she said. "You needn't be so damn self-righteous."

She was right. What a tactless thing to have said. He hated himself for it.

"How are the kids, Harriet?"

"We never had any kids, Ike."

"That's why I thought four hundred dollars a week was a lot for child support."

She bit her lip. Weinstein bit his lip. Then he bit her lip. "Harriet," he said, "I . . . I'm broke. Egg futures are down."

"I see. And can't you get help from your *shiksa?*"

"To you, any girl who's not Jewish is a *shiksa.*"

"Can we forget it?" Her voice was choked with recrimination. Weinstein had a sudden urge to kiss her, or if not her, somebody.

"Harriet, where did we go wrong?"

"We never faced reality."

"It wasn't my fault. You said it was north."

"Reality is north, Ike."

"No, Harriet. Empty dreams are north. Reality is west. False hopes are east, and I think Louisiana is south."

She still had the power to arouse him. He reached out for her, but she moved away and his hand came to rest in some sour cream.

"Is that why you slept with your analyst?" he finally blurted out. His face was knotted with rage. He felt like fainting but couldn't remember the proper way to fall.

"That was therapy," she said coldly. "According to Freud, sex is the royal road to the unconscious."

"Freud said dreams are the road to the unconscious."

"Sex, dreams—you're going to nit-pick?"

"Good-bye, Harriet."

It was no use. Rien à dire, rien à faire. Weinstein left and walked over to Union Square. Suddenly, hot tears burst forth, as if from a broken dam. Hot, salty tears pent up for ages rushed out in an unabashed wave of emotion. The problem was, they were coming out of his ears. Look at this, he thought: I can't even cry properly. He dabbed his ear with a Kleenex and went home.

"No Kaddish for Weinstein"

Mia Farrow and Woody Allen, *Husbands and Wives.*

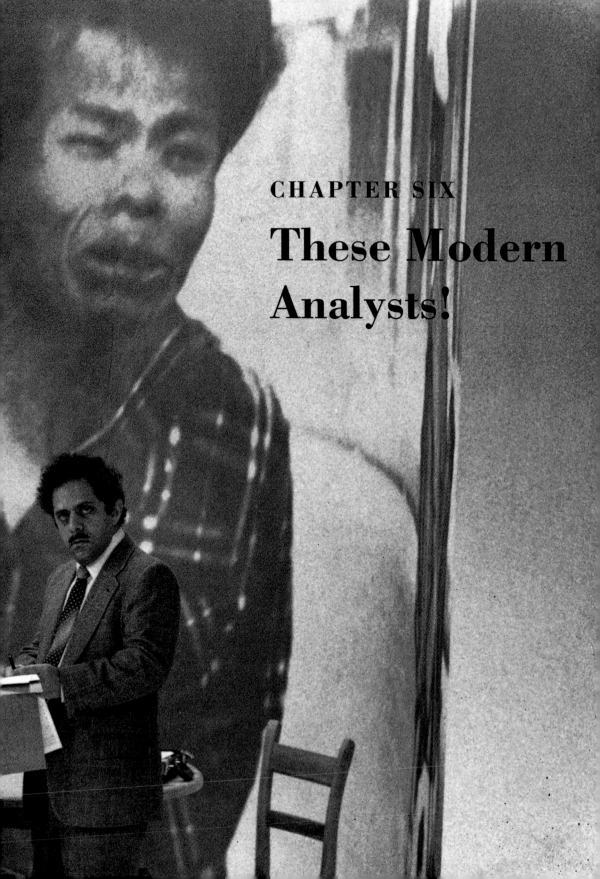

CHAPTER SIX

These Modern Analysts!

I Was in Analysis

Mickey's voice-over: And Freud, another great pessimist. Jesus, I was in analysis for years. Nothing happened. My poor analyst got so frustrated. The guy finally put in a salad bar.

Hannah and Her Sisters

Gabe: Oh, Jesus. Don't do this to me. Why do I hear fifty thousand dollars worth of psychotherapy calling 911?

Husbands and Wives

Annie Hall

Mae Questel, "Oedipus
Wrecks," *New York Stories.*

My Relationship with My Mother

Mother: Look, Sheldon, don't get married.
Sheldon: Mom, I don't wanna discuss it.
Mother: I wanna discuss it. What do you know about that?
     After all, where do you come to a blonde with three
     children? What are you, an astronaut?

_____

Sheldon: I'm fifty years old. I'm a partner in a big law firm,
     you know, I'm very successful and I still haven't
     resolved my relationship with my mother.
Doctor: You still react to her like a small boy. You really
     have to have some sense of humor about it.
Sheldon: I can't. I try, but I can't. You know, I, she just gives
     me a hard time. She's always telling me I look terrible,
     and she's critical. You know, I—listen, what can I
     say? I love her but I wish she would disappear.

     "Oedipus Wrecks," *New York Stories*

His Problem Was Women

Sexually, Weinstein had always felt inadequate. For one thing, he felt short. He was five four in his stocking feet, although in someone else's stocking feet he could be as tall as five six. Dr. Klein, his analyst, got him to see that jumping in front of a moving train was more hostile than self-destructive but in either case would ruin the crease in his pants. Klein was his third analyst. His first was a Jungian, who suggested they try a Ouija board. Before that, he attended "group," but when it came time for him to speak he got dizzy and could only recite the names of the planets. His problem was women, and he knew it. He was impotent with any woman who finished college with higher than a B-minus average. He felt most at home with graduates of typing school, although if the woman did over sixty words a minute he panicked and could not perform.

"No Kaddish for Weinstein"

The Trojan Horse, woodcut, 1632.

O'Shawn Was Obsessed

O'Shawn was obsessed with the Trojan War. He could not believe an army could be so stupid as to accept a gift from its enemy during wartime. Particularly when they got close to the wooden horse and heard giggling inside. This episode seems to have traumatized the young O'Shawn, and throughout his entire life he examined every gift given him very carefully, going so far as to shine a flashlight into a pair of shoes he received on his birthday and calling out, "Anybody in there? Eh? Come on out!"

"The Irish Genius"

Ozymandias Melancholia

Sandy's Analyst: I treated him. He was a complicated patient. He saw reality too clearly. Faulty denial mechanism. Failed to block out the terrible truths of existence. In the end his inability to push away the awful facts of being in the world rendered his life meaningless. Or as one great Hollywood producer said, "Too much reality is not what people want to see." Sandy Bates suffered a depression common to many artists in middle age. In my latest paper for the Psychoanalytic Journal, I have named it Ozymandias Melancholia.

Stardust Memories

I'm a Doctor of the Mind

Victor: You're a doctor?

Dr. Fritz: I'm a doctor of the mind.

Victor: Really? I have terrible emotional problems. Could you
    help me?

Dr. Fritz: You certainly picked an odd time to ask me. I'm in
    the middle of a suicide. . . .

Victor: I'm in love with a girl and she doesn't love me. She
    loves some other guy. I'm just in the way. What do you
    think I ought to do?

Dr. Fritz: Well, why don't you buy a sports car?

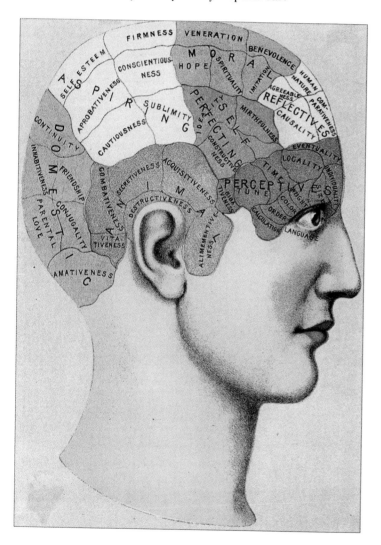

Victor: Sports car?

Dr. Fritz: A nice little two-seater—a French or Italian or German thing. You know they love it. Sign of man's virility. Perhaps you ought to get two maybe.

Victor: I can't drive.

Dr. Fritz: Oh well, so you knock a few people down. The main thing is you get the girl. That's all that matters.

Victor: You know, for a doctor, you sound terribly unethical.

Dr. Fritz: Unethical? What do I give a damn about ethics? Huh? My father, the most beloved gynecologist in Vienna—before they took him away on a morals charge for indecent exposure at the state opera house—he said, and I quote, "Please do not take me away. I won't do it again."

What's New Pussycat?

A Curtain Parted

Pregnant Woman: I just know that I woke up in the middle of the night. And time passed and there were strange shadows. I began having troubling thoughts about my life. Like . . . there was something about it not real. Full of deceptions. At least these deceptions had become so many and so much a part of me now that I couldn't even tell who I really was. And suddenly I began to perspire. I sat up in bed with my heart just pounding. And I looked at my husband next to me and it was as if he was a stranger. When I turned on the light, it woke him up. I asked him to hold me and only after a long time did I finally get my bearings. But for one moment earlier, it was as if a curtain had parted and I could see myself clearly. And I was afraid of what I saw. And what I had to look forward to. And I wondered, I wondered about ending everything.

Another Woman

Manhattan

I Was Going to Kill Myself

I was very depressed for a long time. I was going to kill
myself but, as I said, I was in a strict Freudian analysis and if
you kill yourself, they make you pay for the sessions you miss.

Monologue

Mickey: I went into a store, I bought a rifle. I was gonna . . .
you know, if they told me that I had a tumor, I was going to
kill myself. The only thing that might've stopped me,
might've, is my parents would be devastated. I would, I
woulda' had to shoot them, also, first. And then, I have an
aunt and an uncle, I would have, you know, it would have
been a bloodbath.

Hannah and Her Sisters

An Enormous Abyss

Arthur: I had dropped out of law school when I met Eve. She was very beautiful. Very pale and cool in her black dress . . . with never anything more than a single strand of pearls. And distant. Always poised and distant.

By the time the girls were born . . . it was all so perfect, so ordered. Looking back, of course, it was rigid. The truth is . . . she'd created a world around us that we existed in, where everything had its place, where there was always a kind of harmony. Oh, great dignity. I will say . . . it was like an ice palace.

Then suddenly, one day, out of nowhere . . . an enormous abyss opened up beneath our feet. And I was staring into a face I didn't recognize.

Interiors

Geraldine Page, *Interiors*.

Edvard Munch, *The Scream*, 1893.

Sydney Finkelstein's Hostility

Radio Announcer's Voice: We interrupt this program to bring you a special bulletin. Sydney Finkelstein's hostility has escaped. Finkelstein, a short man with glasses, told police that he had been fighting to hold his anger in for years. And he's very embarrassed that it broke loose while he napped. Police are combing the countryside and warn all citizens to stay indoors.

Stardust Memories

A Notch Below Kafka

Mary: Oh, please, don't psychoanalyze me. I pay a doctor for that.

Ike: Hey, you call that guy you talk to a doctor? I mean, like you don't get suspicious when your analyst calls you up at three in the morning and weeps into the telephone?

Mary: All right, so he's unorthodox. He's a highly qualified doctor.

Ike: He's, he's done a great job on you, you know. Your self-esteem is like a notch below Kafka's.

Manhattan

I believe my consumption has grown worse. Also my asthma. The wheezing comes and goes, and I get dizzy more and more frequently. I have taken to violent choking and fainting. My room is damp and I have perpetual chills and palpitations of the heart. I noticed, too, that I am out of napkins. Will it never stop?

"Selections from the Allen Notebooks"

The Universe Is Expanding

Interestingly, according to modern astronomers, space is
finite. This is a very comforting thought—particularly for
people who can never remember where they have left things.
The key factor in thinking about the universe, however, is that
it is expanding and will one day break apart and disappear.
That is why if the girl in the office down the hall has some
good points but perhaps not all the qualities you require, it's
best to compromise.

"The UFO Menace"

Mother *(to Doctor):* He's been depressed. All of a sudden, he
    can't do anything.
Doctor: Why are you depressed, Alvy?
Alvy: The universe is expanding.
Doctor: The universe is expanding?
Alvy: Well, the universe is expanding, and if it's expanding,
    someday it will break apart and that would be the end
    of everything!
Mother *(shouting):* What is it your business? *(To Doctor)* He
    stopped doing his homework.
Alvy: What's the point?
Mother: What has the universe got to do with it? You're here
    in Brooklyn! Brooklyn is not expanding!
Doctor: It won't be expanding for billions of years yet, Alvy.
    And we've gotta try to enjoy ourselves while we're
    here. Uh?

Annie Hall

Don't Worry About Humanity All the Time

Psychiatrist: What is it that enrages you?
Pregnant Woman: Life.
Psychiatrist: Life?
Pregnant Woman: The universe. The cruelty. The injustice.
    The suffering of humanity. Illness. Aging. Death.
Psychiatrist: All very abstract. Humanity. Don't worry about
    humanity all the time. Get your own life in order. . . .
    We'll continue this tomorrow.

Another Woman

My Analyst Once Suggested Darvon

Linda: Could I get an aspirin?

Allan: I ate all the aspirin. What about Darvon?

Linda: Oh, that's okay. My analyst once suggested Darvon when I had migraines.

Allan: I used to get migraines but my analyst cured me, now I get tremendous cold sores.

Linda: I still do, big ugly ones from tension.

Allan: Yeah, I don't think analysis can help me. I may need a lobotomy.

Linda: With mine on vacation, I feel paralyzed.

Dick: The two of you should get married and move into a hospital.

Allan: You want a Fresca with the Darvon?

Linda: Oh, unless you have apple juice.

Allan: Apple juice and Darvon—it's fantastic together!

Linda: Have you ever had Librium and tomato juice?

Allan: No, I haven't but another neurotic tells me they're unbelieveable.

Play It Again, Sam

Sigmund Freud, April, 1932.

"Oedipus Wrecks," *New York Stories*

Perlemutter's Ego Therapy

By this time, although physically intact, I had developed the
emotional stability of Caligula and, hoping to rebuild my shattered psyche, I volunteered for a program called PET—
Perlemutter's Ego Therapy, named after its charismatic
founder, Gustave Perlemutter. Perlemutter had been a former
bop saxophonist and had come to psychotherapy late in life,
but his method had attracted many famous film stars who
swore that it changed them much more rapidly and in a deeper
way than even the astrology column in *Cosmopolitan*.

A group of neurotics, most of whom had struck out with
more conventional treatment, were driven to a pleasant rural
spa. I suppose I should have suspected something from the
barbed wire and the Dobermans, but Perlemutter's underlings
assured us that the screaming we heard was purely primal.
Forced to sit upright in hardbacked chairs with no relief for
seventy-two straight hours, our resistance gradually crumpled
and it was not long before Perlemutter was reading passages
from *Mein Kampf*. As time passed it was clear that he was a
total psychotic whose therapy consisted of sporadic admoni-
tions to "cheer up."

Several of the more disillusioned ones tried to leave but
to their chagrin found the surrounding fences electrified.

Although Perlemutter insisted he was a doctor of the mind, I noticed he kept receiving phone calls from Yassir Arafat, and were it not for a last-minute raid on the premises by agents of Simon Wiesenthal, there is no telling what might have happened.

"Nefarious Times We Live In"

You'll Like This Group Analysis

Dr. Fritz: I'll see you next Friday.
Michael: But I've only been here for fifteen minutes.
Dr. Fritz: I can't take more than fifteen minutes of your sex
       life at a time. Come to my group analysis meetings.
       I've had great success with it. I want to see how you
       interact with other patients. You'll love it, it's a real
       freak show. If it gets dull, we sing songs.
Michael: If you really think it will help, I'll come.
Dr. Fritz: We'll give it a try. . . . If it fails, we'll try something
       else. I use many unorthodox methods. I've had great
       success locking patients in dark closets.

What's New Pussycat?

"Oedipus Wrecks," *New York Stories*

Then I'm Going to Lourdes

Alvy: Sure, I got nothing till my analyst's appointment.
Annie: Oh, you see an analyst?

Pilgrimage to Lourdes, February, 1958.

Alvy: Yeah, just for fifteen years.

Annie: Fifteen years?

Alvy: Yeah, uh, I'm gonna give him one more year and then
I'm going to Lourdes.

Annie Hall

These Modern Analysts!

"These modern analysts! They charge so much. In my day, for five marks, Freud himself would treat you. For ten marks, he would treat you and press your pants. For fifteen marks, Freud would let you treat him, and that included a choice of any two vegetables. Thirty dollars an hour! Fifty dollars an hour! The Kaiser only got twelve and a quarter for being Kaiser! And he had to walk to work! And the length of treatment! Two years! Five years! If one of us couldn't cure a patient in six months we would refund his money, take him to any musical revue, and he would receive either a mahogany fruit bowl or a set of stainless steel carving knives. I remember you could always tell the patients Jung failed with, as he would give them large stuffed animals."

> "Conversations with Helmholtz"

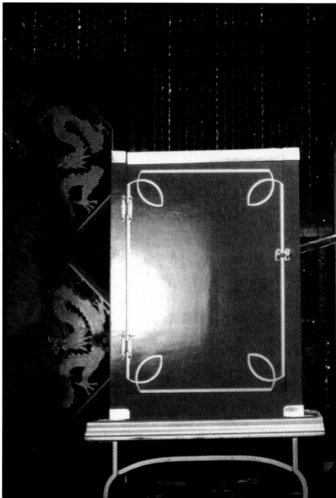

I'm an Analyst, Not a Magician

"Help me. I had a dream last night. I was skipping through a meadow holding a picnic basket and the basket was marked 'Options.' And then I saw there was a hole in the basket."

"Mr. Kugelmass, the worst thing you could do is act out. You must simply express your feelings here, and together we'll analyze them. You have been in treatment long enough to know there is no overnight cure. After all, I'm an analyst, not a magician."

"Then perhaps what I need is a magician," Kugelmass said, rising from his chair. And with that he quit his therapy.

"The Kugelmass Episode"

"Oedipus Wrecks," *New York Stories*

CHAPTER SEVEN

Work, Art and Funnier Jokes

Annie Hall

Art vs. Life

Alvy: You know how you're always trying to get things to come out perfect in art because . . . it's real difficult in life. . . .

Annie Hall

Gabe: I thought your line was great about, uh, "Life doesn't imitate art, it imitates bad television." I mean, it's completely true.

Husbands and Wives

Show Business

Show business is dog eat dog. It's worse than dog eat dog. It's dog doesn't return dog's phone calls.

Crimes and Misdemeanors

The First Time I Ever Acted

I've been in Europe for the last six months making a film called *What's New Pussycat?*, starring Peter O'Toole, Peter Sellers and myself, in that order.

It's the first time in my life that I ever acted in anything like that. I have acted before but I don't count it. Many, many years ago, I was in the nursery school play when I was a child. I played the part of Stanley Kowalski in the school play. We did *Streetcar Named Desire* and I was one of the great five-year-old Stanleys.

I wrote the film and it is an autobiographical movie. . . . As a matter of fact, you should know how I got to Europe in the first place, which is fascinating. I was appearing in Greenwich Village at a coffeehouse on Bleecker Street called the Integration Bagel Shop and Free Car Wash. I was the Master of Ceremonies on the bill. I was on with weird Greenwich Village acts, you know, myself, and an Eskimo vocalist who sang Night and Day six months at a time. A little blonde girl who had a child by a future marriage.

And one night in walks a Mr. Feldman, a producer. He just adored me on sight. He thought I was attractive and sensual and good-looking and just made for motion pictures. He's a little short man with red hair and glasses. . . .

He flies me out to Europe, absolutely all expenses paid. TWA flight. Movie on the flight and everything. Irene Dunne in the life of Amelia Earhardt. You know, I was sitting shaking on the plane.

I meet a girl at my European analyst's. I have to explain this, I was going to a European analyst and that meant a European boy could see my analyst for six months. Neurotic exchange program. . . .

Europe for me, as a matter of fact, was a series of near-misses. I was at a cast party with our cast and I was in the corner and I was playing the vibes, very sexy, like a jazz musician. And a great girl comes up behind me and she says to me, "You play vibes?" I say, "Yeah. It helps me sublimate my sexual tensions." She says, "Why don't you let me help you sublimate your sexual tensions?" So I figure, great, you know, here's a girl who plays vibes.

I turn quickly and ask her out for a date but Peter O'Toole, who's in the movie, asks her out first. Aces me out, you know. She was a beautiful girl so I said to her, "Could you bring a sister for me?" And she did. Sister Maria Teresa.

It was a very slow night. We discussed the New Testament. We agreed that He was extremely well adjusted for an only child.

Monologue

Show Business Is No Life for a Woman

Jerry: Exactly. I knew a girl once, many years ago. . . . I thought she was the one for me—a singer. She came to me at nineteen years old and asked me to help her. I was only about thirty at the time. Naturally, I did everything aboveboard. Did my best for her in a businesslike way. But we couldn't resist a few dinners together. First thing you know, we started getting serious. But I demanded that if we got married, she would have to quit the business. She thought it over, but her drive was too great. She'd have liked to have gotten

Mollie Regan, *Radio Days*.

married, but I couldn't have my wife working saloons and living in hotel rooms. Her name was Rain—Rain Summers. An angel, but consumed with ambition.

Enid: Whatever happened to her?

Jerry: She married Dr. Backwards.

Enid: Who?

Jerry: Dr. Backwards, a fat little vaudevillian—hailed from the Deep South—any word the audience would yell up to him, he'd spell backwards instantly.

Enid: Really?

Jerry: Mississippi . . . antidisestablishmentarianism . . . transportation . . . on a blackboard.

Enid: And he got paid for this?

Jerry: Paid? He was in constant demand. Audiences cheered. Believe me, if I had a man like Backwards I could've retired twice over.

Enid: And she's happy with this Backwards guy?

Jerry: They worked together and fought over top billing. Show business is no life for a woman, or as my father, may he rest in peace, said, "You want a sensible wife who's there for you when you need her—not out doing two a day at the Palace."

The Floating Lightbulb

I'm an Artist

Clown: I'm an artist. Every town we played in, I'd get huge laughs. And here, nothing. No one comes. The few that do just sit there stone-faced.

Irmy: I was very little appreciated myself. None of us were.

Clown: Your specialty is quite different.

Irmy: I don't know about that. I always think you can tell a lot about an audience by how they respond to a sword-swallower.

Clown: Hm, believe me. Nothing is more terrifying than attempting to make people laugh and failing.

Shadows and Fog

John Malkovich, *Shadows and Fog.*

Material for Your First Novel

Rain: I'd better start from the beginning, if I'm going to tell you. My father had this colleague. It was his business partner. . . .

Gabe: This guy was his partner?

Rain: No. Let me tell you from the beginning. It leads up to him. My father's business partner came by my house fairly often. And one day he told me that he was in love with me, right? I was very flattered, to say the least. He was real bright and single and we started this affair. Naturally, we told nobody.

So now I have this friend, Jane. And her parents, they were divorced. Her father, Jerry, developed this mad crush over me, right? And before long, I was seeing both men and instead of being happy, I was just miserable. And I couldn't get my feelings straight so I went to an analyst. I tried for a few months to work things out and then my analyst said that he was gonna stop treating me because he felt it wasn't the thing to do since he was falling in love with me. I was taken with him. I mean, you can imagine. He's quite brilliant.

I started seeing him. I did. I broke off with the other two. But something inside of me told me that he couldn't be very stable, I mean, let alone a good analyst. So I never really let things get too far with him.

Then one night I met Carl and he was very sweet and he really came on to me. I came to my senses and I said to myself, "What am I doing with these older men?" So I cleaned up my act and I've been seeing Carl. But you can see that Richard is so unstable. He really took it badly.

Gabe: My God. You've got material for your first novel, and the sequel and an opera by Puccini here.

Husbands and Wives

Juliette Lewis and Woody Allen, *Husbands and Wives*.

The Lost Generation

I was in Europe many years ago with Ernest Hemingway. Hemingway had just written his first novel. Gertrude Stein and I read it. We said it was a good novel but not a great one, that it needed some work but it could be a fine book. We laughed over it and Hemingway punched me in the mouth.

That winter, Picasso lived on the Rue de Bac. He had just painted a picture of a naked dental hygienist in the middle of the Gobi desert. Gertrude Stein said it was a good picture but not a great one. I said it could be a fine picture and we laughed over it and Hemingway punched me in the mouth.

I remember Scott and Zelda Fitzgerald came home from their wild New Year's Eve party. It was April. Scott had

just written *Great Expectations.* Gertrude Stein and I read it. We said it was a good book but there was no need to have written it because Charles Dickens had already written it. We laughed over it and Hemingway punched me in the mouth.

That winter we went to Spain to see Manolete fight. He looked to be eighteen and Gertrude Stein said, no, he was nineteen but that he only looked to be eighteen. I said, "Sometimes a boy of eighteen will look nineteen whereas, other times, a nineteen-year-old can easily look eighteen, and that's the way it is with a true Spaniard." We laughed over that and Gertrude Stein punched me in the mouth.

Monologue

Left:
Pablo Picasso, *Gertrude Stein,*
1905.

Above:
Ernest Hemingway and
Antonio Ordoñez, ca. late
1950s.

In a London Pub with Willie Maugham

Rain. Six straight days of rain. Then fog. I sit in a London pub with Willie Maugham. I am distressed, because my first novel, *Proud Emetic*, has been coolly received by the critics. Its one favorable notice, in the *Times*, was vitiated by the last sentence, which called the book "a miasma of asinine clichés unrivaled in Western letters."

Maugham explains that while this quote can be interpreted many ways, it might be best not to use it in the print ads. Now we stroll up Old Brompton Road, and the rains come again. I offer my umbrella to Maugham and he takes it, despite the fact he already has an umbrella. Maugham now carries two umbrellas while I run along beside him.

"One must never take criticism too seriously," he tells

me. . . . Maugham pauses to buy and open a third umbrella. "In order to be a writer," he continues, "one must take chances and not be afraid to look foolish. I wrote *The Razor's Edge* while wearing a paper hat. In the first draft of *Rain*, Sadie Thompson was a parrot. We grope. We take risks. All I had when I began *Of Human Bondage* was the conjunction 'and.' I knew a story with 'and' in it could be delightful. Gradually the rest took shape."

A gust of wind lifts Maugham off his feet and slams him into a building. He chuckles. Maugham then offers the greatest advice anyone could give a young author: "At the end of an interrogatory sentence, place a question mark. You'd be surprised how effective it can be."

"Reminiscences: Places and People"

Husbands and Wives

155

Tell Funnier Jokes

Walsh: He's pretentious. His filming style is too fancy. His insights are shallow and morbid. I've seen it all before. They try to document their private suffering and fob it off as art.

Taylor: What does he have to suffer about? Doesn't the man know he's got the greatest gift anyone could have? The gift of laughter?

OG: Hey, look, I'm a superintelligent being. By earth standards I have an IQ of sixteen hundred and even I can't understand what you expected from that relationship with Dorrie. . . .

Sandy: But shouldn't I stop making movies and do something that counts, like helping blind people or becoming a missionary or something?

OG: Let me tell you, you're not the missionary type. You'd never last. And, incidentally, you're also not Superman, you're a comedian. You want to do mankind a service? Tell funnier jokes.

Stardust Memories

Laughter, remaining subconscious in its manifest realm (or as Freud put it, when it comes out of the mouth), often works best after something funny has happened. This is why the death of a friend almost never gets a chuckle but a funny hat does.

"Woody, the Would-Be Critic," *The New York Times*

Can't Anybody Write Funny Anymore?

Lester: All right, look, this story on the homeless, it's too long.
I want five pages out of it. Make sure he gets five real pages
out of it. This guy tells his secretary to type tighter. He doesn't
take anything out of it. It's stupid. And I want Joe Hansen off
the show. He's not funny. He doesn't write funny. He has cancer, I'll send him flowers. I want him off. Can't anybody write
funny anymore? Am I supposed to write everything myself?
Direct it myself, produce it myself? Look at those people out
there! Look at them! They're looking for something funny!
You're giving them straight lines! Their lives are straight lines
already! They're waiting for something funny!

Crimes and Misdemeanors

Manhattan

Stardust Memories

I Wrote a Science-Fiction Film

Professor Leon Speciman postulates a civilization in outer space that is more advanced than ours by approximately fifteen minutes. This, he feels gives them a great advantage over us, since they needn't rush to get to appointments.

"The UFO Menace"

I wrote a science-fiction film which I'll tell you about. It's ten after four in the afternoon and everybody in the world mysteriously falls asleep. Just like that—they're driving cars, whatever they're doing—bang,—they go to sleep. The Russians, the Chinese, the Americans and the whole world sleeps for exactly one hour, till ten after five. They wake up at ten after five and, mysteriously upon awakening, everybody in the world finds himself in the pants business.

Stay with this because it's brilliant.

Everybody's making cuffs and flies and cutting velvet. And a space ship lands from another planet and men get out with jackets and shirts and black socks. No trousers at all. They say, "Are the pants ready?"

And we say, "No, could you come back Thursday?"

They say they must have them because they're going to a wedding.

And we work diligently and make pants constantly. They come to get them and when they come to pick them up they leave us with socks, handkerchiefs, pillow cases and soiled linen. They say, "Do it."

The President of the United States goes on television and says, "An alien super power from outer space with superior intelligence is bringing us their laundry, and they're foiled because they traveled 117 million light-years to pick it up and they forget their ticket."

Monologue

As a general rule, careful on-the-scene investigations disclose that most "unidentified" flying objects are quite ordinary phenomena, such as weather balloons, meteorites, satellites, and even once a man named Lewis Mandelbaum, who blew off the roof of the World Trade Center. A typical "explained" incident is the one reported by Sir Chester Ramsbottom, on June 5, 1961, in Shropshire: "I was driving along the road at two a. m. and saw a cigar-shaped object that seemed to be tracking my car. No matter which way I drove, it stayed with me, turning sharply at right angles. It was a fierce, glowing red, and in spite of twisting and turning the car at high speed I could not lose it. I became alarmed and began sweating. I let out a shriek of terror and apparently fainted, but awoke in a hospital miraculously unharmed." Upon investigation, experts determined that the "cigar-shaped object" was Sir Chester's nose. Naturally, all his evasive actions could not lose it, since it was attached to his face.

"The UFO Menace"

The Great Scandinavian Playwright

Perhaps no other writer has created more fascinating and complex females than the great Scandinavian playwright Jorgen Lovborg, known to his contemporaries as Jorgen Lovborg. Tortured and embittered by his agonizing relationships with the opposite sex, he gave the world such diverse and unforgettable characters as Jenny Angstrom in *Geese Aplenty* and Mrs. Spearling in *A Mother's Gums*. Born in Stockholm in 1836, Lovborg (originally Lövborg, until, in later years, he removed the two dots from above the 'o' and placed them over his eyebrows) began writing plays at the age of fourteen. His first produced work, brought to the stage when he was sixty-one, was *Those Who Squirm*, which drew mixed notices from the critics, although the frankness of the subject matter (cheese fondling) caused conservative audiences to blush. Lovborg's work can be divided into three periods. First came the series of plays dealing with anguish, despair, dread, fear and loneliness (the comedies); the second group focused on social changes (Lovborg was instrumental in bringing about safer methods of weighing herring); finally, there were the six great tragedies written just before his death, in Stockholm in 1902, when his nose fell off, owing to tension.

"Lovborg's Women Considered"

A Dramatist of Zero Promise

Lunching yesterday on chicken in ichor—a house specialty at my favorite midtown restaurant—I was forced to listen to a playwright acquaintance defend his latest opus against a set of notices that read like a Tibetan *Book of the Dead.* Drawing tenuous connections between Sophocles' dialogue and his own, Moses Goldworm wolfed down his vegetable cutlet and raged like Carrie Nation against the New York theater critics. I, of course, could do nothing more than offer a sympathetic ear and assure him that the phrase "a dramatist of zero promise" might be interpreted in several ways.

"A Giant Step for Mankind"

Zelig

It's All Luck

Sandy: I think I'm a little drunk. What do you want me to say? I was the kid in the neighborhood who told jokes, right?

Jerry: Yeah.

Sandy: So, so—we, you know, we live in a society that puts a big value on jokes, you know? If you think of it this way—if I had been an Apache Indian, those guys didn't need comedians at all, right? So, I'd be out of work.

Jerry: So? Oh, come on, that doesn't help me feel any better, you know?

Sandy: I don't know what to say, I got such a headache. You know it's luck. It's all luck. I was just lucky. I'm the first to admit, I was a lucky bum. If I was not born in Brooklyn, if I had been born in Poland, or Berlin, I'd be a lampshade today, right?

Stardust Memories

The Earl of Sandwich Invented the Sandwich

1718: Birth of the Earl of Sandwich to upper-class parents. . . .

1725-35: Attends school . . . comes in contact with cold cuts for the first time and displays an unusual interest in thinly sliced strips of roast beef and ham. . . .

1736: Enters Cambridge University, at his parents' behest, to pursue studies in rhetoric and metaphysics, but displays little enthusiasm for either. In constant revolt against everything academic, he is charged with stealing loaves of bread and performing unnatural experiments with them. Accusations of heresy result in his expulsion.

1738: He meets Nell Smallbore, a greengrocer's daughter, and they marry. She is to teach him all he will ever know about lettuce.

1741: Living in the country on a small inheritance, he works day and night, often skimping on meals to save money for food. His first completed work—a slice of bread, a slice of bread on top of that, and a slice of turkey on top of both—fails miserably. . . .

1750: In the spring, he exhibits and demonstrates three consecutive slices of ham stacked on one another . . . he is sent for by Voltaire.

1758: His growing acceptance by opinion-makers wins him a commission by the Queen to fix "something special" for a luncheon with the Spanish ambassador. He works day and night, tearing up hundreds of blueprints, but finally—at 4:17 a.m., April 27, 1758—he creates a work consisting of several strips of ham enclosed, top and bottom, by two slices of rye bread. In a burst of inspiration, he garnishes the work with mustard. . . .

1769: Living on a country estate, he is visited by the greatest men of his century: Haydn, Kant, Rousseau and Ben Franklin stop at his home, some enjoying his remarkable creations at table, others ordering to go.

1778: Though aging physically, he still strives for new forms and writes in his diary, "I work long into the cold nights and am toasting everything now in an effort to keep warm." Later that year, his open hot roast beef sandwich creates a scandal with its frankness.

1792: He develops genu varum, which he fails to treat in time, and succumbs in his sleep. He is laid to rest in Westminster Abbey, and thousands mourn his passing. At his funeral, the great German poet Holderlin sums up his achievements with undisguised reverence: "He freed mankind from the hot lunch. We owe him so much."

"Yes, But Can the Steam Engine Do This?"

Greg Wakabayashi, *Blueprint: Plan, Elevation, and Axonometric Views of the Sandwich,* 1993.

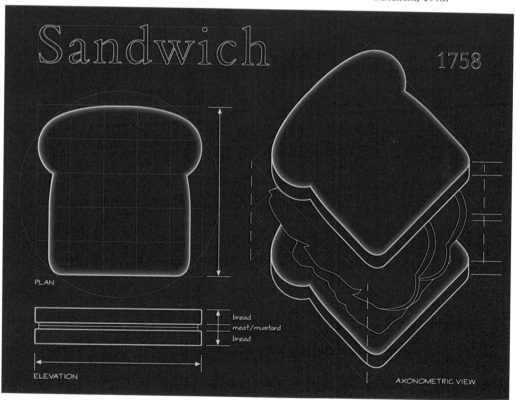

A Group of Biologists
Discovered the Fake Ink Blot

Then, in 1921, a group of biologists meeting in Hong Kong to buy suits discovered the fake ink blot. It had long been a staple of the Oriental repertoire of diversions, and several of the later dynasties retained power by their brilliant manipulation of what appeared to be a spilled bottle and an ugly ink stain, but was in reality a tin blot.

The first ink blots, it was learned, were crude, constructed to eleven feet in diameter, and fooled nobody.

However, with the discovery of the concept of smaller sizes by a Swiss physicist, who proved that an object of a particular size could be reduced in size simply by "making it smaller," the fake ink blot came into its own.

It remained in its own until 1934, when Franklin Delano Roosevelt removed it from its own and placed it in someone else's. Roosevelt utilized it cleverly to settle a strike in Pennsylvania, the details of which are amusing. Embarrassed leaders of both labor and management were convinced that a bottle of ink had been spilled, ruining someone's priceless Empire sofa. Imagine how relieved they were to learn it was all in fun. Three days later the steel mills were reopened.

"The Discovery and Use of the Fake Ink Blot"

Trading Pelts and Whale Blubber

Arriving in Boston, Entwhistle meets Margaret Figg, a comely New England schoolteacher whose specialty is baking bread and then placing it on her head. Enticed, Entwhistle marries her and the two open a small store, trading pelts and whale blubber for scrimshaw in an ever-increasing cycle of meaningless activity. . . .His small trading post will go on to become a giant modern department store, and when he dies at eighty-five, from a combination of smallpox and a tomahawk in the skull, he is happy.

"By Destiny Denied"

We're on a Waiting List

High Macher: Good Afternoon. I'm the Grand Exalted High
Macher of Raspar, a nonexistent but real-sounding
country. Yes. We're on a waiting list. As soon as
there's an opening on the map, we're next. It's rough
on a new country. Do you realize the entire population is still packed in crates?

Phil Moscowitz: Good luck. I'm sure you'll get your country
on the globe.

High Macher: Thank you. I'm hoping for something
between Spain and Greece. It's really much warmer
there.

What's Up, Tiger Lily?

*Hercules Supporting the
Celestial Sphere.*
Detail, from the Sphere series.
Woven by or at the order of
Georg Wezeler, after a cartoon
attributed to Bernaert van
Orley. Brussels, ca. 1520-
1530.

He Played for the Old St. Louis Cardinals

Bill Kern: Today's story is about a baseball player. His name was Kirby Kyle, a lean southpaw from Tennessee. He played for the old St. Louis Cardinals. He threw fast and he had a good curve ball and all the hitters knew it. He was a kid with a great future. But one day he went hunting. He loved to hunt. Just like his father and his father's father. Chasing a rabbit, he stumbled and his rifle went off. The bullet entered his leg. Two days later, it was amputated. They said he would never pitch again. But the next season he was back. He had one leg, but he had something more important. He had heart.

The following winter, another accident cost Kirby Kyle an arm. Fortunately, not his pitching arm. He had one leg and one arm but more than that he had heart.

The next winter, going after duck, his gun misfired. He was blind. But instinct told him where to throw the baseball. Instinct and heart.

The following year, Kirby Kyle was run over by a truck and killed.

The following season he won eighteen games in the big league in the sky.

This has been Bill Kern with another favorite sports legend.

Radio Days

Brian Mannian, *Radio Days*.

I Got a Job on Madison Avenue

I was thrown out of college and when I was thrown out of
college, I got a job on Madison Avenue in New York. A real
died-in-the-wool advertising agency on Madison Avenue wanted a man to come in and they'd pay him $95 a week to sit in
their office and look Jewish. They wanted to prove to the outside world that they would hire minority groups, you know. So
I was the one they hired. I was the show Jew with the agency. I
tried to look Jewish desperately. Used to read my memos from
right to left all the time. They fired me finally because I took
off too many Jewish holidays.

Monologue

I Don't Need a Job

Cliff: I don't need a job. Didn't I get honorable mention at
that festival in . . . in . . . in . . .?
Wendy: In Cincinnati? The Cincinnati Documentary Film
Festival? This is what you're clinging to? Everybody
got honorable mention who showed up.

Crimes and Misdemeanors

Nice Job

Michael: Did you find a job?
Victor: Yeah. I got something at the striptease. I help dress
and undress the girls.
Michael: Nice job.
Victor: Twenty francs a week.
Michael: Not very much.
Victor: It's all I could afford.

What's New Pussycat?

Smitten by Hard Times

And it came to pass that a man who sold shirts was smitten by hard times. Neither did any of his merchandise move nor did he prosper. And he prayed and said, "Lord, why hast thou left me to suffer thus? All mine enemies sell their goods except I. And it's the height of the season. My shirts are good shirts. Take a look at this rayon. I got button-downs, flare collars, nothing sells. Yet I have kept thy commandments. Why can I not earn a living when mine younger brother cleans up in children's ready-to-wear?"

And the Lord heard the man and said, "About thy shirts. . . . "

"Yes, Lord," the man said, falling to his knees.

"Put an alligator over the pocket."

"Pardon me, Lord?"

"Just do what I'm telling you. You won't be sorry."

And the man sewed on to all his shirts a small alligator symbol and lo and behold, suddenly his merchandise moved like gangbusters, and there was much rejoicing while amongst his enemies there was wailing and gnashing of teeth, and one said, "The Lord is merciful. He maketh me to lie down in green pastures. The problem is, I can't get up."

"The Scrolls"

Organized Crime in America

It is no secret that organized crime in America takes in over forty billion dollars a year. This is quite a profitable sum, especially when one considers that the Mafia spends very little for office supplies. Reliable sources indicate that the Cosa Nostra laid out no more than six thousand dollars last year for personal stationery, and even less for staples. Furthermore, they have one secretary who does all the typing, and only three small rooms for headquarters, which they share with the Fred Persky Dance Studio.

"A Look at Organized Crime"

The Best Damn Burglar You Ever Saw

Sure, I stole. Why not? Where I grew up, you had to steal to eat. Then you had to steal to tip. Lots of guys stole fifteen percent, but I always stole twenty, which made me a big favorite among the waiters. On the way home from a heist, I'd steal some pajamas to sleep in. Or if it was a hot night, I'd steal underwear. It was a way of life. . . .

Woolworth's, 1942.

I was the best damn burglar you ever saw. People talk about Raffles, but Raffles had his style and I had mine. I had lunch with Raffles's son once. Nice guy. We ate at the old Lindy's. He stole the pepper mill. I stole the silverware and napkins. Then he took the ketchup bottle. I took his hat. He got my umbrella and tiepin. When we left we kidnapped the waiter. It was quite a haul.

"Confessions of a Burglar"

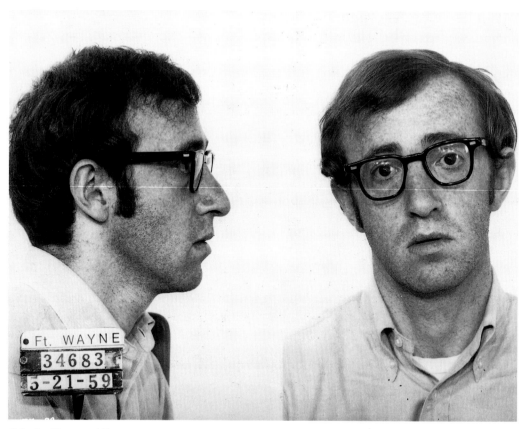

Take the Money and Run

He Never Made the Ten-Most-Wanted List

Louise: He's been very depressed. I think if he'd been a successful criminal, he would've felt better. You know, he never made the Ten-Most-Wanted list. It's very unfair voting. It's who you know.

Narrator: Although he doesn't make the Ten-Most-Wanted list, he does win Gangster of the Year Award and is asked to speak at many luncheons and universities.

Take the Money and Run

Advice to the Average Homeowner

What advice would I give to the average homeowner to protect himself against burglars? Well, the first thing is to keep a light on in the house when you go out. It must be at least a sixty-watt bulb; anything less and the burglar will ransack the house, out of contempt for the wattage. Another good idea is to keep a dog, but this is not foolproof. Whenever I was about to rob a house with a dog in it, I threw in some dog food mixed with Seconal. If that didn't work, I'd grind up equal parts of chopped meat and a novel by Theodore Dreiser. If it happens that you are going out of town and must leave your house unguarded, it's a good idea to put a cardboard silhouette of yourself in the window. Any silhouette will do. A Bronx man once placed a cardboard silhouette of Montgomery Clift in his window and then went to Kutscher's for the weekend. Later, Montgomery Clift himself happened to walk by and saw the silhouette, which caused him great anxiety. He attempted to strike up a conversation, and when it failed to answer for seven hours, Clift returned to California and told friends that New Yorkers were snobbish.

If you surprise an intruder in the act of burglarizing your home, do not panic. Remember, he is as frightened as you are. One good device is to rob him. Seize the initiative and relieve the burglar of his watch and wallet. Then he can get into your bed while you make a getaway. Trapped by this defense, I once wound up living in Des Moines for six years with another man's wife and three children, and only left when I was fortunate enough to surprise another burglar, who took my place.

"Confessions of a Burglar"

I Do It for the Money

Playboy: One critic has suggested that your technique of turning personal misfortune into comedy helps you "get even with the world." Is he right?

Allen: No. I do it for the money. You can't get even with the world. It takes too long and too many lawyers.

Playboy interview

On Frugality

As one goes through life, it is extremely important to conserve
funds, and one should never spend money on anything foolish,
like pear nectar or a solid gold hat. Money is not everything,
but it is better than having one's health. After all, one cannot
go into a butcher shop and tell the butcher, "Look at my great
suntan, and besides I never catch colds," and expect him to
hand over any merchandise. (Unless, of course, the butcher is
an idiot.) Money is better than poverty, if only for financial
reasons. . . . The point is, we all need a nest egg to fall back
on, but not while wearing a good suit.

Finally, let us bear in mind that it is easier to spend two
dollars than to save one. And for God's sake don't invest
money in any brokerage firm in which one of the partners is
named Frenchy.

"The Early Essays"

I Got No Cash Flow

Ike: That's not the point. Money, what's money got to
do . . .? I've got enough for a year. If I live like Mahatma
Gandhi, I'm fine. My accountant says that I did this at a very
bad time. My stocks are down. I'm cash poor or something. I
got no cash flow. I'm not liquid or something's not flowing. I
know it. But they got a language all their own, these guys . . .
plus, I got two alimonies and I got child support and I got—
you know, I gotta cut down. I'm gonna have to give up my
apartment, I'm not gonna be able to do the tennis lessons, I'm
not gonna pick the checks up at dinner or, you know, I won't
be able to take the Southhampton house . . . plus, I'll probably
have to give my parents less money. You know, this is gonna
kill my father. He's not gonna be able to get as good a seat in
the synagogue. This year he's gonna be in the back, away from
God, far from the action.

Manhattan

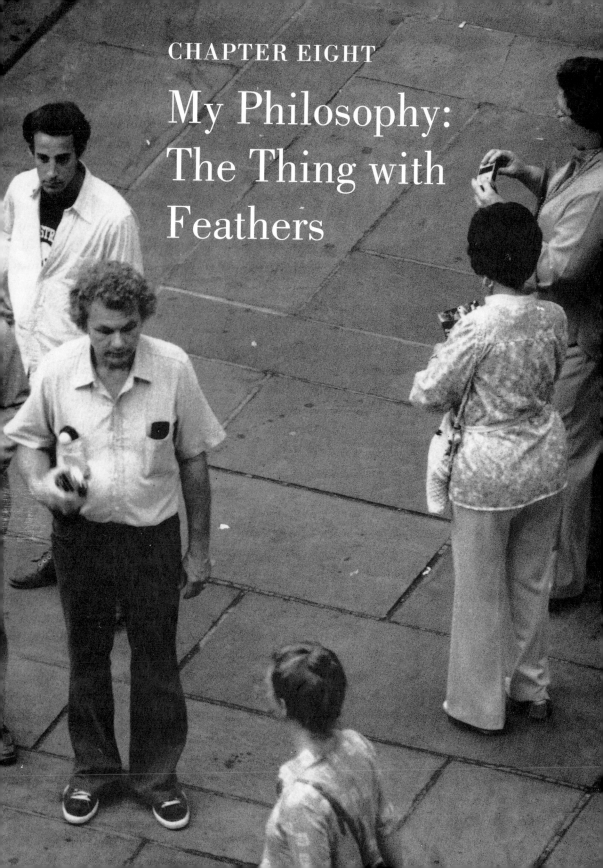

CHAPTER EIGHT

My Philosophy: The Thing with Feathers

The Big Questions

Mickey's voice-over: Millions of books written on every conceivable subject by all these great minds and, in the end, none of them knows anything more about the big questions of life than I do. I read Socrates. You know, this guy used to knock off little Greek boys. What the hell's he got to teach me? And, and Nietzsche with his, with his Theory of Eternal

"The Famous Skating
Sextette" at Thos. Healy's
Crystal Carnival Ice Rink.

Recurrence. He said that the life we live, we're gonna live
over and over again the exact same way for all eternity. Great.
That means I'll have to sit through the Ice Capades again. It's
not worth it.

Hannah and Her Sisters

A Quintessential Human Paradox

An air of imminent apocalypse hung over the shoe department like a wet tarpaulin as Carmen Pinchuck handed his box to Blanche Mandelstam and said, "I'd like to return these loafers. They're too small."

"Do you have a sales slip?" Blanche countered, trying to remain poised, although she confessed later that her world had suddenly begun falling apart. ("I can't deal with people since the accident," she has told friends. Six months ago, while playing tennis, she swallowed one of the balls. Since then her breathing has become irregular.)

"Er, no," Pinchuck replied nervously. "I lost it." (The central problem of his life is that he is always misplacing things. Once he went to sleep and when he awoke the bed was missing.) Now, as customers lined up behind him impatiently, he broke into a cold sweat.

"You'll have to have it O.K.'d by the floor manager," Blanche said, referring Pinchuck to Mr. Dubinsky, whom she had been having an affair with since Halloween. (Lou Dubinsky, a graduate of the best typing school in Europe, was a genius until alcohol reduced his speed to one word per day and he was forced to go to work in a department store.)

"Have you worn them?" Blanche continued, fighting back tears. The notion of Pinchuck in his loafers was unbearable to her. "My father used to wear loafers," she confessed. "Both on the same foot."

Pinchuck was writhing now. "No," he said. "Er—I mean yes. I had them on briefly, but only while I took a bath."

"Why did you buy them if they're too small?" Blanche asked, unaware that she was articulating a quintessential human paradox.

"By Destiny Denied"

Is Knowledge Knowable?

Is knowledge knowable? If not, how do we know this?

"Spring Bulletin"

In formulating any philosophy, the first consideration must always be: What can we know? That is, what can we be sure we know, or sure that we know we knew it, if indeed it is at all knowable. Or have we simply forgotten it and are too embarrassed to say anything? Descartes hinted at the problem when he wrote: "My mind can never know my body, although it has become quite friendly with my legs." By "knowable," incidentally, I do not mean that which can be known by perception of the senses, or that which can be grasped by the mind, but more that which can be said to be Known or to possess a Knownness or Knowability, or at least something you can mention to a friend.

Can we actually "know" the universe? My God, it's hard enough finding your way around Chinatown. The point, however, is: Is there anything out there? And must they be so noisy?

Finally, there can be no doubt that the one characteristic of "reality" is that it lacks essence. That is not to say it has no essence, but merely lacks it. (The reality I speak of here is the same one Hobbes described, but a little smaller.) Therefore the Cartesian dictum "I think, therefore I am" might better be expressed "Hey, there goes Edna with a saxophone."

"My Philosophy"

Cloquet Hated Reality

Cloquet hated reality but realized it was still the only place to get a good steak.

"The Condemned"

Woody Allen and Diane
Keaton, *Manhattan.*

Jackson Pollock, *Untitled,*
  (ca. 1939–42).

182

The Hideous Lonely Emptiness of Existence

Allan: That's quite a lovely Jackson Pollock, isn't it?
Woman: Yes it is.
Allan: What does it say to you?
Woman: It restates the negativeness of the universe. The hideous lonely emptiness of existence. Nothingness. The predicament of Man forced to live in a barren, Godless eternity like a tiny flame flickering in an immense void with nothing but waste, horror and degradation forming a useless bleak straitjacket in a black absurd cosmos.
Allan: What are you doing Saturday night?
Woman: Committing suicide.
Allan: What about Friday night?

Play It Again, Sam

I'm Talking About the Universe

Peter: What branch of physics are you involved with?

Lloyd: Something more terrifying than blowing up the planet.

Peter: Is anything more terrifying than world destruction?

Lloyd: The knowledge that it doesn't matter either way. It's all random. Originating aimlessly out of nothing and eventually vanishing forever. I'm not talking about the world. I'm talking about the universe. All space, all time, just . . . a temporary convulsion. And I get paid to prove it.

Peter: Do you feel sure of that when you see all those millions of stars?

Lloyd: I think it's as beautiful as you do and vaguely evocative of some deep truth that always just keeps slipping away. But then my professional perspective overcomes me. A less wishful, more penetrating view of it. And I understand it for what it truly is. Haphazard . . . morally neutral and unimaginably violent.

Peter: Look, we shouldn't have this conversation. I have to sleep alone tonight.

September

The Body Is More Dependable

Ah, God, how the mind boggles when it turns to moral or ethical considerations! Better not to think too much. Rely more on the body—the body is more dependable. It shows up for meetings, it looks good in a sports jacket, and when it really comes in handy is when you want to get a rubdown.

"The Condemned"

I Felt My Spirit Leave My Body

Mr. Albert Sykes reports the following experience: "I was sitting having biscuits with some friends when I felt my spirit leave my body and go make a telephone call. For some reason, it called the Moscowitz Fiber Glass Company. My spirit then returned to my body and sat for another twenty minutes or so, hoping nobody would suggest charades. When the conversation turned to mutual funds, it left again and began wondering around the city. I am convinced that it visited the Statue of Liberty and then saw the stage show at Radio City Music Hall. Following that, it went to Benny's Steak House and ran up a tab of sixty-eight dollars. My spirit then decided to return to my body, but it was impossible to get a cab. Finally, it walked up Fifth Avenue and rejoined me just in time to catch the late news. I could tell that it was reentering my body, because I felt a sudden chill, and a voice said, 'I'm back. You want to pass me those raisins?'

"This phenomenon has happened to me several times since. Once, my spirit went to Miami for a weekend, and once it was arrested for trying to leave Macy's without paying for a tie. The fourth time, it was actually my body that left my spirit, although all it did was get a rubdown and come right back."

Spirit departure was very common around 1910, when many "spirits" were reported wandering aimlessly around India searching for the American Consulate. The phenomenon is quite similar to transubstantiation, the process whereby a person will suddenly dematerialize and rematerialize somewhere else in the world. This is not a bad way to travel, although there is usually a half-hour wait for luggage.

"Examining Psychic Phenomena"

Since Turning Fifty

Marion: Can I help you?

Hope (crying): I'm sorry. I don't know why I'm so emotional. I was just looking at that picture there and, it just made me feel so sad.

Marion: Oh, but this is a very optimistic work. You know, I saw the original of this once. In fact, its title is "Hope." I think of all the paintings Klimt did during that period, this is the most positive.

Hope: I'm sorry. Are you an artist?

Marion: Yes, I—well, I used to do some painting when I was younger. I was absolutely in love with this whole school.

Hope: It's funny, just this morning, I was thinking about how I missed painting. I'd like to get back into it.

Marion: Really? . . .

Marion (voice-over): We left the store and walked along together. I wanted to know her better without getting pushy. We talked about art, and the discussion seemed to cheer her a little. We stopped at a gallery and spent some time marveling at the pictures, and I took a chance and invited her to lunch. I was excited when she accepted. She suggested a little out-of-the-way place that was charming and quite private. We ordered a bottle of wine, although she hardly touched it, being pregnant. The result was that I wound up drinking most of it . . . and while I really wanted to find out about her, it was me who wound up doing most of the talking.

Marion: Fifty? I didn't think anything turning thirty. Everybody said I would. Then they said I'd be crushed turning forty. But they were wrong. I didn't give it a second thought. Then they said I'd be traumatized when I hit fifty. And they were right. I'll tell you the truth. I don't think I've ever recovered my balance since turning fifty.

Another Woman

Gustav Klimt, *Expectation*, 1905-9.

Consciousness Expanding Material

I do not use—you should know this about me, too—any sort of consciousness expanding material. My body will not tolerate that. I took a puff of the wrong cigarette at a fraternity dance once. The cops had to get me. I broke two teeth trying to give a hickey to the Statue of Liberty.

Monologue

On Youth and Age

The true test of maturity is not how old a person is but how he reacts to awakening in the midtown area in his shorts. What do years matter, particularly if your apartment is rent-controlled? The thing to remember is that each time of life has its appropriate rewards, whereas when you're dead it's hard to find the light switch. The chief problem about death, incidentally, is the fear that there may be no afterlife—a depressing thought, particularly for those who have bothered to shave. Also, there is the fear that there is an afterlife but no one will know where it's being held. On the plus side, death is one of the few things that can be done as easily lying down.

Consider, then: Is old age really so terrible? Not if you've brushed your teeth faithfully! And why is there no buffer to the onslaught of the years? Or a good hotel in downtown Indianapolis? Oh, well.

In short, the best thing to do is behave in a manner befitting one's age. If you are sixteen or under, try not to go bald. On the other hand, if you are over eighty, it is extremely good form to shuffle down the street clutching a brown paper bag and muttering: "The Kaiser will steal my string." Remember, everything is relative, or should be. If it's not, we must begin again.

"The Early Essays"

It's Hell Turning Older

Diane: It's hell turning older. Especially when you feel twenty-one inside. All the strengths that have sustained you all through your life just vanish one by one. You study your face in the mirror and notice something is missing. Then you realize it's your future.

September

The Horrible and the Miserable

Alvy: I've a very pessimistic view of life. You should know this about me if we're gonna go out, you know. I feel that life is divided up into the horrible and the miserable . . . the horrible would be like, uh, I don't know, terminal cases, you know? And blind people, crippled. I don't know how they get through life. It's amazing to me . . . and the miserable is everyone else. That's all. So, when you go through life you should be grateful that you're miserable. You're very lucky— to be miserable.

Annie Hall

Diane Keaton and Woody Allen, *Annie Hall.*

Good and Bad People

It seemed the world was divided into good and bad people.
The good ones slept better, Cloquet thought, while the bad
ones seemed to enjoy the waking hours much more.

"The Condemned"

The Problem of Evil

As always, at the time of Needleman's death he was at work
on several things. He was creating an Ethics, based on his
theory that "good and just behavior is not only more moral but
could be done by phone." Also, he was halfway through a new
study of semantics, proving (as he so violently insisted) that
sentence structure is innate but whining is acquired. Finally,
yet another book on the Holocaust. This one with cutouts.
Needleman had always been obsessed by the problem of evil
and argued quite eloquently that true evil was only possible if
its perpetrator was named Blackie or Pete. His own flirtation
with National Socialism caused a scandal in academic cir-
cles, though despite everything from gymnastics to dance
lessons, he could not master the goose step.

"Remembering Needleman"

Moral Implications

I have been asked if I was aware of the moral implications of
what I was doing. As I told the tribunal at Nuremberg, I did
not know that Hitler was a Nazi. The truth is that for years I
thought he worked for the phone company.

"The Schmeed Memoirs"

The Randomness of the Cosmos

My good friend Jacques Monod spoke often of the randomness
of the cosmos. He believed everything in existence occurred
by pure chance with the possible exception of his breakfast,
which he felt certain was made by his housekeeper. Naturally,
belief in a divine intelligence requires tranquillity. But this
does not free us from human responsibilities. Am I my brother's keeper? Yes. Interestingly, in my case I share that honor
with the Prospect Park Zoo. Feeling godless then, what we
have done is made technology God. And yet can technology
really be the answer when a brand-new Buick, driven by my
close associate Nat Zipsky, winds up in the window of
Chicken Delight causing hundreds of customers to scatter?
My toaster has never once worked properly in four years. I
follow the instructions and push two slices of bread down in
the slots and only seconds later they rifle upwards. Once they
broke the nose of a woman I loved very dearly. Are we count-
ing on nuts and bolts and electricity to solve our problems?
Yes, the telephone is a good thing, and the refrigerator, and
the air-conditioner. But not every air-conditioner. Not my sister Henny's, for instance. Hers makes a loud noise and still
doesn't cool. When the man comes over to fix it, it gets worse.
Either that or he tells her she needs a new one. When she
complains, he says not to bother him. This man is truly alienated. Not only is he alienated but he can't stop smiling.

"My Speech to the Graduates"

Existential Nausea

A feeling of nausea swept over him as he contemplated the
implications of his action. This was an existential nausea,
caused by his intense awareness of the contingency of life,
and could not be relieved with an ordinary Alka-Seltzer.
What was required was an Existential Alka-Seltzer—a product sold in many Left Bank drugstores. It was an enormous
pill, the size of an automobile hubcap, that, dissolved in
water, took away the queasy feeling induced by too much
awareness of life. Cloquet had also found it helpful after eating Mexican food.

"The Condemned"

The Purple Rose of Cairo

His Worst Beliefs Are Realized

Judah: My murder story has a very strange twist. Let's say
there's this man who's very successful. He has everything . . .

And after the awful deed is done, he finds that he's
plagued by deep-rooted guilt. Little sparks of his religious background, which he'd rejected, are suddenly
stirred up. He hears his father's voice. He imagines
God is watching his every move. Suddenly, it's not an
empty universe at all but a just and moral one and he's
violated it. Now he's panic-striken. He's on the verge of
mental collapse. An inch away from confessing the
whole thing to the police. And then one morning he
awakens. The sun is shining and his family is around
him and mysteriously, the crisis is lifted. He takes his
family on a vacation to Europe and as the months pass
he finds he's not punished. In fact, he prospers. The

killing gets attributed to another person, a drifter who has a number of other murders to his credit, so, what the hell, one more doesn't even matter. Now he's scot-free. His life is completely back to normal. Back to his protected world of wealth and privilege.

Cliff: Yes, but can he ever really go back?

Judah: People carry sins around with them. I mean, maybe once in a while he has a bad moment, but it passes. And with time, all fades.

Cliff: Yeah, but, so then his worst beliefs are realized.

Judah: I said it was a chilling story, didn't I?

Cliff: I don't know. I think very few guys could actually live with something like that on their consciences.

Judah: What do you mean? People carry awful deeds around with them. What do you expect him to do, turn himself in? I mean, this is reality. In reality, we rationalize. We deny or we couldn't go on living.

Cliff: Well, here's what I'd do. I'd have him turn himself in. Then your story assumes tragic proportions because in the absence of a God or something, he's forced to assume responsibility for himself. Then you have tragedy.

Judah: But that's fiction. That's movies. You see too many movies. I'm talking about reality. I mean, if you want a happy ending, you should go see a Hollywood movie.

Crimes and Misdemeanors

Taking the Fifth

Weinstein's so-called friends had all knuckled under to the House Un-American Activities Committee. Blotnick was turned in by his own mother. Sharpstein was turned in by his answering service. Weinstein had been called by the committee and admitted he had given money to the Russian War Relief, and then added, "Oh, yes, I bought Stalin a dining-room set." He refused to name names but said if the committee insisted he would give the heights of the people he had met at meetings. In the end he panicked and instead of taking the Fifth Amendment, took the Third, which enabled him to buy beer in Philadelphia on Sunday.

"No Kaddish for Weinstein"

193

All I See Is Human Suffering

Manager: Sandy, we've got to talk about the new picture.

Sandy: What do you want me to say? I don't want to make funny movies anymore. They can't force me to . . . I don't feel funny. I look around the world and all I see is human suffering.

Manager: Human suffering doesn't sell tickets in Kansas City.

Press Agent: They want laughs in Kansas City. They've been working in the wheat fields all day.

Stardust Memories

Annie Hall

Woody Allen and Mia Farrow, *Broadway Danny Rose.*

You've Got to Suffer a Little, Too

Danny: Well, you know, my Uncle Morris, the famous diabet-
ic from Brooklyn, used to say, "If you hate yourself,
then you hate your work."

Tina: I sleep at night. It's you that's got the ulcer.

Danny: Yeah, I got an ulcer, but you know, it may be, it may
be a good thing there. You know what my philosophy
of life is? That it's important to have some laughs, no
question about it, but you've got to suffer a little, too.
Because otherwise, you miss the whole point of life.
And that's how I feel.

Tina: Yeah. You know what my philosophy of life is?

Danny: Ach, I can imagine.

Tina: It's over quick, so have a good time. You see what you
want, go for it. Don't pay any attention to anybody
else. And do it to the other guy first, 'cause if you
don't, he'll do it to you.

Danny: This is a philosophy of life? This sounds like the
screenplay to Murder Incorporated.

Broadway Danny Rose

195

And It All Goes on Forever

Gina: To me the city at night is so cold and dark and empty. This must be what it's like in outer space.

Kleinman: I never cared for outer space.

Gina: But you're in outer space. We're just this big, round ball floating in space. . . . You can't tell which way is up.

Kleinman: You think that's good? I'm a man who likes to know which way is up and which way is down and where's the bathroom.

Gina: You think there's life on any of those billions of stars out there?

Kleinman: I personally don't know. Although I hear there may be life on Mars, but the guy that told me is only in the hosiery business.

Gina: And it all goes on forever.

Kleinman: How can it go on forever? Sooner or later it must stop. Right? I mean sooner or later it must end and there's, er—a wall or something—be logical.

Gina: Are you saying the universe is finite?

Kleinman: I'm not saying anything. I don't want to get involved.

Death (A Play)

But It All Passes So Quickly

Kleinman: It's so pretty. The stars are beginning to come out. I've never taken the time to look. The fog is just breaking a tiny bit.

Irmy: You see that very bright star up in that direction? For all we know that star could've disappeared a million years ago. And it's taken the light from it a million years to reach us.

Kleinman: I don't understand. Are you saying that star is not there? That's a very disquieting thought, you know? Because when I see something with my own eyes, I like to know that it's really there. Otherwise, a person could sit down in a chair and break his neck. You

Woody Allen and Mia Farrow, *Shadows and Fog.*

have to be able to rely on things. It's important. You
know who has these thoughts all the time is Schultz
the tailor. He thinks nothing is real and that everything exists only in the dream of a dog.

Irmy: Well, but this is real, isn't it? And beautiful. Think
about it for a minute. We're two strangers, out in the
night and it's just so peaceful and quiet. Suddenly
there's a clearing in the fog and you can see right out
into the stars. But doesn't this moment just seem perfect?

Kleinman: Yes, but you know it passes so quickly. Now the
fog is starting to go back in. Everything's always moving all the time. Everything's constantly in motion. So
it's no wonder that I'm nauseous.

Shadows and Fog

Human Happiness

Professor Levy: We are all faced throughout our lives with
agonizing decisions, moral choices. Some are on a grand
scale. Most of these choices are on lesser points. But we
define ourselves by the choices we have made. We are, in
fact, the sum total of our choices. Events unfold so unpre-
dictably, so unfairly. Human happiness does not seem to have
been included in the design of creation. It is only we, with our
capacity to love, who give meaning to the indifferent universe.
And yet, most human beings seem to have the ability to keep
trying and even to find joy from simple things like their family, their work and from the hope that future generations might
understand more.

Crimes and Misdemeanors

Woody Allen with his son,
Satchel, during the filming of
Alice, 1990.

I Just Didn't Realize I Was Happy

Mickey: If I have a brain tumor, I don't know what I'm gonna do.

Gail: You don't have a brain tumor. He didn't say you have a brain tumor.

Mickey: No, naturally, they're not gonna tell you, because, well, you know, sometimes the weaker ones will panic.

Gail: But not you.

Mickey: Oh God! Do you hear a buzzing? Is there a buzzing?

Gail: Mickey, come on, we got a show to do!

Mickey: I can't keep my mind on the show.

Gail: But there's nothing wrong with you!

Mickey: If there's nothing wrong with me then why does he want me to come back for tests?

Gail: Well, he has to rule out certain things.

Mickey: Like what? What?

Gail: I don't know. Cancer, I—

Mickey: Don't say that! I don't want to hear that word! Don't mention that word while I'm in the building.

Gail: But you don't have any symptoms!

Mickey: You—I got the classic symptoms of a brain tumor!

Gail: Two months ago you thought you had a malignant melanoma.

Mickey: Naturally, I, I—Do you know I—The sudden appearance of a black spot on my back!

Gail: It was on your shirt.

Mickey: How was I to know? Everyone was pointing back there.

Gail: Come on, we've got to make some booking decisions.

Mickey: I can't. I can't think of it. This morning I was so happy, you know. Now I, I don't know what went wrong.

Gail: You were miserable this morning. We got bad reviews, terrible ratings, the sponsors are furious—

Mickey: No, I was happy, but I just didn't realize I was happy.

Hannah and Her Sisters

The Idea Was Not to Expect Too Much Out of Life

Gabe *(voice-over, reading):* "The heart raged and demanded, grew melancholy and confused and to what end? To articulate what nitwit strategy? Procreation? It told him how mind-boggling numbers of sperm competed for a single egg. It was not the other way around.

"Of course men would make love at any place with any number of women, including total strangers, while females were more selective. They were, in each case, catering to the demands of only one small egg, while each male had millions and millions of frantic sperm screaming wildly, 'Let us out. Please, let us out, now!'

"It was like those desperate ads in the personals columns with a dozen requirements and, if they were not enough, there was added, 'Must be a non-smoker.'

"Feldman longed for a woman who attracted him physically and had a quick sense of humor and a love of sports equal to his; and a love of classical music and a fondness for Bach and balmy climates. In short, he wanted himself, but as a pretty woman.

"Pepkin married and raised a family. He led a warm domestic life. Placid, but dull.

"Knapp was a swinger. He eschewed nuptial ties and bedded five different women a week. Students, housewives, nurses, actresses, a doctor, a salesgirl, you name it, it held Knapp between its legs.

"Pepkin, from the calm of his fidelity, envied Knapp.

"Knapp, lonely beyond belief, envied Pepkin.

"What happened when the honeymoon ended? Did desire really grow with the years, or did familiarity cause partners to long for other lovers? Was the notion of ever-deepening romance a myth we'd grown up on like simultaneous orgasm? The only time Rifkin and his wife had a simultaneous orgasm was when they got their divorce.

"Maybe, in the end, the idea was not to expect too much out of life."

Husbands and Wives

The Predicament of Modern Man

More than any other time in history, mankind faces a cross-roads. One path leads to despair and utter hopelessness. The other, to total extinction. Let us pray we have the wisdom to choose correctly. I speak, by the way, not with any sense of futility, but with a panicky conviction of the absolute mean-inglessness of existence which could easily be misinterpreted as pessimism. It is not. It is merely a healthy concern for the predicament of modern man. (Modern man is here defined as any person born after Nietzsche's edict that "God is dead," but before the hit recording, "I Wanna Hold Your Hand.") This "predicament" can be stated one of two ways, though certain linguistic philosophers prefer to reduce it to a mathe-matical equation where it can be easily solved and even car-ried around in a wallet.

"My Speech to the Graduates"

O'Shawn was definitely a pessimist, and felt that no good could come to mankind until they agreed to lower their body temperature from 98.6, which he felt was unreasonable.

"The Irish Genius"

The Thing with Feathers

How wrong Emily Dickinson was! Hope is not "the thing with feathers." The thing with feathers has turned out to be my nephew. I must take him to Zurich.

"Selections from the Allen Notebooks"

Emily Dickinson

CHAPTER NINE

I Am Two
with Nature

Mia Farrow and Woody Allen, *Zelig*.

The Country Makes Me Nervous

Alvy: Well, I can't live—We can't have this discussion all
the time. The country makes me nervous. There's . . . you get
crickets and it's quiet. . . . There's no place to walk after dinner, and . . . there's the screens with the dead moths behind
them, and . . . you got the Manson family possible. . . .

Annie Hall

Sonja: Isn't nature incredible?
Boris: Ah, to me nature is, I don't know, spiders . . . and
bugs, and . . . then, then big fish eating little fish,
and then, then plants eating, ah, plants and animals
eating . . . it's like an enormous restaurant. That's the
way I see it.

Love and Death

A Moth Ate My Sports Jacket

I came home one night, some months ago, and I went to the
closet in my bedroom and a moth ate my sports jacket. He
was laying on the floor, nauseous. It's a yellow and green
striped jacket, you know. A little fat moth laying there, groan-
ing. Part of the sleeve hanging out of his mouth. I gave him
two plain brown socks. I said, "Eat one now and eat one in a
half-hour."

Monologue

The Ant and the Grasshopper

Take the case of the ant and the grasshopper: The grasshopper played all summer while the ant worked and saved. When
winter came, the grasshopper had nothing, but the ant com-
plained of chest pains. Life is hard for insects. And don't
think mice are having any fun, either.

"The Early Essays"

We know that the most advanced computer in the world does
not have a brain as sophisticated as that of an ant. True, we
could say that of many of our relatives but we only have to put
up with them at weddings or special occasions.

"My Speech to the Graduates"

Thought: Why does man kill? He kills for food. And not only
for food: frequently there must be a beverage.

"Selections from the Allen Notebooks"

Interiors

The Esthetics of Perfection

Nights of loneliness led me to ponder the esthetics of perfection. Is anything in nature actually "perfect" with the exception of my Uncle Hyman's stupidity? Who am I to demand perfection? I, with my myriad faults. I made a list of my faults, but could not get past:

    1) Sometimes forgets his hat.

"The Lunatic's Tale"

On Tripping Through a Copse and Picking Violets

This is no fun at all, and I would recommend almost any other
activity. Try visiting a sick friend. If this is impossible, see a
show or get into a nice warm tub and read. Anything is better
than turning up in a copse with one of those vacuous smiles
and accumulating flowers in a basket. Next thing you know,
you'll be skipping to and fro. What are you going to do with
the violets once you get them, anyhow? "Why, put them in a
vase," you say. What a stupid answer. Nowadays you call the
florist and order by phone. Let him trip through the copse,
he's getting paid for it. That way, if an electrical storm comes
up or a beehive is chanced upon, it will be the florist who is
rushed to Mount Sinai.

    Do not conclude from this, incidentally, that I am insen-
sitive to the joys of nature, although I have come to the con-
clusion that for sheer fun it is hard to beat forty-eight hours at
Foam Rubber City during the high holidays. But that is
another story.

"The Early Essays"

Mia Farrow and Woody Allen, *Broadway Danny Rose.*

Rene Magritte,
The Third Dimension,
1942.

On Seeing a Tree in Summer

Of all the wonders of nature, a tree in summer is perhaps the
most remarkable, with the possible exception of a moose
singing "Embraceable You" in spats. Consider the leaves, so
green and leafy (if not, something is wrong). Behold how the
branches reach up to heaven as if to say, "Though I am only a
branch, still I would love to collect Social Security."

"The Early Essays"

The Lesser Ballets

The Sacrifice: A melodic prelude recounts man's relation to the earth and why he always seems to wind up buried in it. The curtain rises on a vast primitive wasteland, not unlike certain parts of New Jersey. Men and women sit in separate groups and then begin to dance, but they have no idea why and soon sit down again. Presently a young male in the prime of life enters and dances a hymn to fire. Suddenly it is discovered he is on fire, and after being put out he slinks off. Now the stage becomes dark, and Man challenges Nature—a stirring encounter during which Nature is bitten on the hip, with the result that for the next six months the temperature never rises above thirteen degrees.

Scene two opens, and Spring still has not come, although it is late August and no one is quite sure when to set the clocks ahead. The elders of the tribe meet and decide to propitiate Nature by sacrificing a young girl. A maiden is selected. She is given three hours to report to the outskirts of town, where she is told they are having a weenie roast. When the girl appears that night, she asks where all the frankfurters are. She pleads pathetically, telling them that she is not that good a dancer. The villagers insist, and, as the music builds relentlessly, the girl spins in a frenzy, achieving sufficient centrifugal force to hurl her silver fillings across a football field. Everybody rejoices, but too soon, for not only does Spring fail to come but two of the elders get subpoenaed in a mail-fraud charge.

A Day in the Life of a Doe: Unbearably lovely music is heard as the curtain rises, and we see the woods on a summer afternoon. A fawn dances on and nibbles slowly at some leaves. He drifts lazily through the soft foliage. Soon he starts coughing and drops dead.

"A Guide to Some of the Lesser Ballets"

One of the Most Beautiful Summer Nights

Andrew: Remember that night right in these woods. This spot, to be exact.

Ariel: Of course I remember. It was one of the most beautiful summer nights I've ever seen.

Andrew: I think of that night often, very often, and when I do I want to kill you. Kill you, or kill myself, but more often, you.

Ariel: Why didn't you act? I wanted you to . . . I wanted you to take me and make love to me.

Andrew: I didn't know!

Ariel: How could you not see? It was written all over me.

Andrew: If you knew how much I wanted to grab you and make love to you.

Ariel: You'd have had a great time, believe me.

Andrew: Don't say that! I didn't think you wanted me to!

Ariel: I wanted your hands all over me.

Andrew: I thought I'd offend you . . . we'd been out maybe three times—tops. You were this diplomat's daughter, fine upbringing . . . raised by nuns, finishing schools. . . . We were not in love. It was pure animal sex. Lust. I'd have given my right arm to undress and just do every awful thing to you anyone could think of.

Ariel: That's just what I was in the mood for.

Andrew: I know, I know. I missed an opportunity. It's so sad! I've regretted it since! It's the saddest thing in life—a missed opportunity. And most infuriating because later, a month later, after you had gone away to Europe, only then I found out that you were and had been sleeping with everybody! Everybody!

Ariel: Not everybody. Well, maybe it was everybody.

Andrew: I wouldn't have been the first, I would've been the twenty-first! Poets, actors, bankers, the infield of the Chicago White Sox!

Ariel: I was not one of your shrinking, mousy, inhibited, little virgins.

Andrew: That's the understatement of the century. . . .

Ariel: I think amongst all the love affairs I was running through in those days you were the one person who could have stopped me.

Andrew: I could have?

Ariel: I was beginning to care for you. Who knows what would have happened if we had made love that night. The moment was so perfect and people learn things about themselves through lovemaking that they never dreamed of.

Woody Allen and Mia Farrow,
A Midsummer Night's Sex Comedy.

A Midsummer's Night Sex Comedy

211

I Shot a Moose Once

Here's a story you're not going to believe. I shot a moose once. I was hunting in upstate New York and I shot a moose. And I strap him onto the fender of my car, and I'm driving home along the West Side Highway. But what I didn't realize was that the bullet did not penetrate the moose. It just creased his scalp, knocking him unconscious. And I'm driving through the Holland Tunnel and the moose woke up. So I'm driving with a live moose on my fender and the moose is signaling for a turn. And there's a law in New York State against driving with a conscious moose on your fender, Tuesdays, Thursdays and Saturdays. And I'm very panicky.

And then it hits me—some friends of mine are having a costume party. I'll go. I'll take the moose. I'll ditch him at the party. It wouldn't be my responsibility. So I drive up to the party and I knock on the door. The moose is next to me. My host comes to the door. I say, "Hello, you know the Solomons." We enter. The moose mingles. Did very well. Scored. Some guy was trying to sell him insurance for an hour and a half.

Twelve o'clock comes, they give out prizes for the best costume of the night. First prize goes to the Berkowitzes, a married couple dressed as a moose. The moose comes in second. The moose is furious! He and the Berkowitzes lock antlers in the living room. They knock each other unconscious.

Now, I figure, here's my chance. I grab the moose, strap him on my fender, and shoot back to the woods. But I've got the Berkowitzes. So I'm driving along with two Jewish people on my fender. And there's a law in New York State, Tuesday, Thursday and especially Saturday. . . .

The following morning, the Berkowitzes wake up in the woods in a moose suit. Mr. Berkowitz is shot, stuffed and mounted at the New York Athletic Club. And the joke is on them, because it's restricted.

Monologue

212

Radio Days

CHAPTER TEN

Religion: To God, I'm the Loyal Opposition

Do You Believe in God?

I was having tea and cracknels with my uncle at a fine restaurant. Suddenly my uncle put a question to me. "Do you believe in God?" he asked. "And if so, what do you think He weighs?" So saying, he took a long and luxurious draw on his cigar and, in that confident, assured manner he has cultivated, lapsed into a coughing fit so violent I thought he would hemorrhage.

"I do not believe in God," I told him. "For if there is a God, then tell me, Uncle, why is there poverty and baldness? Why do some men go through life immune to a thousand mortal enemies of the race, while others get migraines that last for weeks? Why are our days numbered and not, say, lettered? Answer me, Uncle. Or have I shocked you?"

I knew I was safe in saying this, because nothing ever shocked the man. Indeed, he had seen his chess tutor's mother raped by Turks and would have found the whole incident amusing had it not taken so much time.

"Good nephew," he said, "there is a God, despite what you think, and He is everywhere. Yes! Everywhere!"

"Everywhere, Uncle? How can you say that when you don't even know for sure we exist? True, I am touching your wart at this moment, but could that not be an illusion? Could not all life be an illusion? Indeed, are there not certain sects of holy men in the East who are convinced that nothing exists outside their minds except for the Oyster Bar at Grand Central Station? Could it not be simply that we are alone and aimless, doomed to wander in an indifferent universe, with no hope of salvation, nor any prospect except misery, death and the empty reality of eternal nothing?"

I could see that I made a deep impression on my uncle with this, for he said to me, "You wonder why you're not invited to more parties! Jesus, you're morbid!" He accused me of being nihilistic and then said, in that cryptic way the senile have, "God is not always where one seeks Him, but I assure you, dear nephew, He is everywhere. In these cracknels, for instance." With that, he departed, leaving me his blessing and a check that read like the tab for an aircraft carrier.

"Notes from the Overfed"

How Do You Know He Exists?

Maybe God did exist and maybe He didn't, but somewhere in that city there were sure a lot of guys who were going to try and keep me from finding out.

My first lead was Rabbi Itzhak Wiseman, a local cleric who owed me a favor for finding out who was rubbing pork on his hat. I knew something was wrong when I spoke to him because he was scared. Real scared.

"Of course there's a you-know-what, but I'm not even allowed to say his name or He'll strike me dead, which I could never understand why someone is so touchy about having his name said."

"You ever see Him?"

"Me? Are you kidding? I'm lucky I get to see my grand-children."

"Then how do you know He exists?"

"How do I know? What kind of question is that? Could I get a suit like this for fourteen dollars if there was no one up there? Here, feel the gabardine—how can you doubt?"

"You got nothing more to go on?"

"Hey, what's the Old Testament? Chopped liver? How do you think Moses got the Israelites out of Egypt, with a smile and a tap dance? Believe me, you don't part the Red Sea with some gismo from Korvettes."

"Mr. Big"

Erinnerung
1914

Chagall
914

218

Do You Pray Ever?

Irmy: Are you a religious person?

Kleinman: No. You're the second person tonight to ask me that. The doctor, may he rest in peace, wanted to know.

Irmy: Do you pray ever?

Kleinman: My people pray in a different language. I never understood it. For all I know, they were requesting their own trouble.

Shadows and Fog

Marc Chagall, *Remembrance,*
ca. 1918.

The Faithful Do Not Question

. . . And Abraham woke in the middle of the night and said to his only son, Isaac, "I have had a dream where the voice of the Lord sayeth that I must sacrifice my only son, so put your pants on." And Isaac trembled and said, "So what did you say? I mean when He brought this whole thing up?"

"What am I going to say?" Abraham said. "I'm standing there at two a.m. in my underwear with the Creator of the Universe. Should I argue?"

"Well, did He say why He wants me sacrificed?" Isaac asked his father.

But Abraham said, "The faithful do not question. Now let's go because I have a heavy day tomorrow."

And Sarah, who heard Abraham's plan, grew vexed and said, "How doth thou know it was the Lord and not, say, thy friend who loveth practical jokes, for the Lord hateth practical jokes and whosoever shall pull one shall be delivered into the hands of his enemies whether they can pay the delivery charge or not." And Abraham answered, "Because I know it was the Lord. It was a deep, resonant voice, well modulated, and nobody in the desert can get a rumble in it like that."

And Sarah said, "And thou art willing to carry out this senseless act?" But Abraham told her, "Frankly yes, for to question the Lord's word is one of the worst things a person can do, particularly with the economy in the state it's in."

And so he took Isaac to a certain place and prepared to sacrifice him but at the last minute the Lord stayed Abraham's hand and said, "How could thou doest such a thing?"

And Abraham said, "But Thou said—"

"Never mind what I said," the Lord spake. "Doth thou listen to every crazy idea that comes thy way?" And Abraham grew ashamed. "Er—not really, no."

"I jokingly suggest thou sacrifice Isaac and thou immediately runs out to do it."

And Abraham fell to his knees, "See, I never know when You're kidding."

And the Lord thundered, "No sense of humor. I can't believe it."

"But doth this not prove I love Thee, that I was willing to donate my only son on Thy whim?"

And the Lord said, "It proves that some men will follow

any order no matter how asinine as long as it comes from a resonant, well-modulated voice."

And with that, the Lord bid Abraham get some rest and check with Him tomorrow.

"The Scrolls"

What's One of the First Things That God Asks?

Professor Levy: Now, then, the first thing that happened to the early Israelites was that they conceived a God who cares. He cares, but at the same time, He also demands that you behave morally. But here comes the paradox. What's one of the first things that God asks? That God asks Abraham to sacrifice his only son, his beloved son, to Him. In other words, in spite of millennia of efforts, we have not succeeded to create a really and entirely loving image of God. This was beyond our capacity to imagine.

Crimes and Misdemeanors

Decorative doors of the Ark of the Torah Scroll, Italy, 19th century.

221

A Crisis of Faith

Religion too has unfortunately let us down. Miguel de Unamuno writes blithely of the "eternal persistence of consciousness," but this is no easy feat. Particularly when reading Thackeray. I often think how comforting life must have been for early man because he believed in a powerful, benevolent Creator who looked after all things. Imagine his disappointment when he saw his wife putting on weight. Contemporary man, of course, has no such peace of mind. He finds himself in the midst of a crisis of faith. He is what we fashionably call "alienated." He has seen the ravages of war, he has known natural catastrophes, he has been to singles bars.

"My Speech to the Graduates"

A Leap of Faith

Jack: Here's a thoughtful-looking man. What are your views on divine matter?

Kleinman: Excuse me. Me?

Jack: I'm asking if you believe in God.

Kleinman: That's the third time tonight someone asked me that question. I would love to. I know I would be much happier.

Jack: Yeah, but you can't.

Kleinman: I can't, no. It's just . . . you know . . .

Jack: You doubt His existence and you can't make the leap of faith necessary.

Kleinman: Listen, I can't make the leap of faith necessary to believe in my own existence.

Shadows and Fog

An Orthodox Scholar of the Torah

Rabbi Zwi Chaim Yisroel, an Orthodox scholar of the Torah and a man who developed whining to an art unheard of in the West, was unanimously hailed as the wisest man of the

Renaissance by his fellow-Hebrews, who totaled a sixteenth of
one percent of the population. Once, while he was on his way
to synagogue to celebrate the sacred Jewish holiday commem-
orating God's reneging on every promise, a woman stopped
him and asked the following question: "Rabbi, why are we not
allowed to eat pork?"

"We're not?" the Rev said incredulously. "Uh-oh."

This is one of the few stories in all Hassidic literature
that deals with Hebrew law. The rabbi knows he shouldn't eat
pork; he doesn't care, though, because he likes pork. Not only
does he like pork; he gets a kick out of rolling Easter eggs. In
short, he cares very little about traditional Orthodoxy and
regards God's covenant with Abraham as "just so much chin
music." Why pork was proscribed by Hebraic law is still
unclear, and some scholars believe that the Torah merely suggested not eating pork at certain restaurants.

"Hassidic Tales"

An Ethical Crisis

A big vodka company wanted to do a prestige ad—they originally wanted Noel Coward for it but he was not available. He
had acquired the rights to *My Fair Lady* and he was removing
the music and lyrics and making it back into *Pygmalion.*
. . . I'll tell you how they got my name. It was on a list in
Eichmann's pocket when they picked him up.

And I'm sitting home one night . . . and the phone rings.
A voice on the other end says, "How would you like to be this
year's vodka man?"

I said, "No. I'm an artist. I do not do commercials. I
don't pander. I don't drink vodka and, if I did, I wouldn't
drink your product."

He said, "Too bad, it pays fifty thousand dollars."

I said, "Hold on. I'll put Mr. Allen on the phone."

And I was caught here in an ethical crisis. Should I
advertise a product I don't actually use? This is the problem,
because I'm not a drinker, my body will not tolerate spirits,
really. I had two martinis New Year's Eve and I tried to hijack
an elevator and fly it to Cuba.

In the past, whenever I had any sort of emotional problem, I used to consult with my analyst all the time. This is
public knowledge. . . . I was in a strict Freudian analysis for
a long time. My analyst died two years ago and I never realized it.

And now, whenever I have any sort of problem, I consult
with my spiritual counselor, who, in my case, is my rabbi. I
called him up on the phone and I laid the proposition on him
and he said, "Don't do it because it's illegal and immoral to
advertise a product that you don't use just for the money."

I said okay and I passed the ad up. I must say it took
great courage at the time because I needed the money. I was
writing and I needed to be freed creatively. I was working on
a nonfiction version of the Warren Report.

A month later, I'm leafing through *Life* magazine and I
see a photo of Monique Van Buren in a slim bikini and she's
on the beach in Jamaica and there, next to her, with a cool
vodka in his hand, is my rabbi.

So I call him up on the phone, you know, and he puts me
on hold and, what happened was, he wanted to go into show
business. He had done a late night prayer on television and

Marc Chagall, *The Praying Jew*, 1923.

he was in the middle of the Twenty-Third psalm and he tried
to ad lib. He tried to name the Ten Commandments and he
couldn't think of them quickly; instead he named the seven
dwarfs. He's got a discotheque now with his colleagues—
they're topless rabbis, no skullcap on.

Monologue

God Is Silent

Human freedom for Needleman consisted in being aware of
the absurdity of life. "God is silent," he was fond of saying,
"now if only we can get Man to shut up."

"Remembering Needleman"

On location with the crew from *Bananas*. Left to right:
Ralph Rosenbloom, editor; Hank Polansky, production
assistant; Fred Gallo, first assistant director; Mickey
Rose, co-writer; Ed Wittstein, set design; and Jack
Grossberg, producer.

Some Kind of Higher Power

Ben: It's a fundamental difference in the way we view the world. You see it as harsh and empty of values and pitiless, and I couldn't go on living if I didn't feel with all my heart a moral structure with real meaning and forgiveness and some kind of higher power. Otherwise there's no basis to know how to live. . . .

Crimes and Misdemeanors

God Doesn't Play Dice

TV Scientist *(on television to audience):* Einstein was then celebrating the seventieth birthday anniversary and there was a colloquium given for him. And he said: "God doesn't play dice with the universe."
Gabe: No, he just plays hide-and-seek.

Husbands and Wives

We're All Guilty in the Eyes of God

Danny: What are you talking about? Guilt is important. It's important to feel guilty. Otherwise you, you know, you're capable of terrible things. You know. It's very important to be guilty. I'm guilty all the time and I never did anything. You know? My rabbi, Rabbi Perlstein, used to say we're all guilty in the eyes of God.
Tina: You believe in God?
Danny: No, no. But, uh, I'm guilty over it.

Broadway Danny Rose

A Berserk Evangelist

Years ago, my mother gave me a bullet. I put it in my breast pocket. Two years after that, I was walking down the street when a berserk evangelist heaved a Gideon Bible out a hotel room window, hitting me in the chest. The Bible would've gone through my heart if it wasn't for the bullet.

Monologue

I'm Plagued by Doubts

Do I believe in God? I did until my mother's accident. She fell on some meat loaf, and it penetrated her spleen. She lay in a coma for months, unable to do anything but sing "Granada" to an imaginary herring. Why was this woman in the prime of life so afflicted—because in her youth she dared to defy convention and got married with a brown paper bag on her head? And how can I believe in God when just last week I got my tongue caught in the roller of an electric typewriter? I am plagued by doubts. What if everything is an illusion and nothing exists? In that case, I definitely overpaid for my carpet. If only God would give me some clear sign! Like making a large deposit in my name in a Swiss bank.

"Selections from the Allen Notebooks"

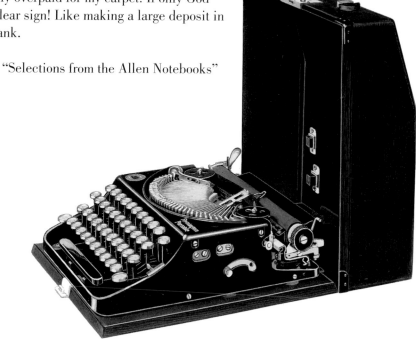

229

Alice's Confession

Alice: My sister's been right about so many things. I am too much like Mom. Sometimes I think I'm not raising my children with the right values. That I'm spoiling them. Not exposing them to the things that matter most. When I was young, I wanted to be a saint. I used to pray with my arms outstretched because it was more painful. And I could feel closer to God. I wanted to spend my life helping people, taking care of the sick and the old people. I was never happier than when I got the chance to help out that way. What happened? Where did that part of me go?

Alice

To God I'm the Loyal Opposition

Sandy: And, you know, the whole point of the movie is that nobody is saved.

Walsh: Sandy, this is an Easter film. We don't need a movie by an atheist.

Sandy: To you—to you I'm an atheist . . . to God I'm the loyal opposition.

Stardust Memories

Sharon: My father takes after his Aunt May. She rejected the Bible because it had an unbelievable central character.

Crimes and Misdemeanors

A Tremendous Religious Conflict

I used to go to New York University, a long time ago, which is in Greenwich Village. That's where I started. I was in love in my freshman year but I did not marry the first girl I fell in love with because there was a tremendous religious conflict at the time. She was an atheist and I was an agnostic. We didn't know which religion not to bring the children up in.

I bummed around for a long time and I met my wife and we got married against my parents' wishes. We were married in Long Island, in New York. We were married by a reformed rabbi in Long Island—a very reformed rabbi—a Nazi.

Monologue

I'll Make a Deal with God

Mickey's voice-over: I'm dying! I'm dying! I know it! There's a spot on my lungs! All right now, take it easy, will you? It's not on your lungs. It's on your ear. No, it's the same thing, isn't it? Oh jeez, I can't sleep! Oh, God, there's a tumor in my head the size of a basketball! Now I keep thinking I can feel it every time I blink! Oh, Jesus! He, he wants me to do a brain scan to confirm what he already suspects. . . . Look . . . I'll make a deal with God. Let it just be my ear, okay? I'll go deaf and blind in one eye maybe. But I don't want a brain operation! Once they go into my skull, I'll wind up like the guy with the wool cap who delivers for the florist!

Hannah and Her Sisters

Aaron the High Priest filling the Menorah. Hebrew manuscript, late 13th century.

Moses Was Right

Boris: Who are you?

Angel *(off-screen):* I am an angel of God.

Boris: You're kidding!

Angel: Fear not, Boris . . . you have led a just life and, at the last minute before the execution, the Emperor plans to pardon you.

Boris: Really?

Angel: He will make a great personal show of his generosity, and you will have learned your lesson . . . but you will not be executed.

Boris *(to himself):* Then, there is a God. Incredible! Moses was right! He that abideth in truth . . . will have Frankincense and Myrrh smeared on his gums in abundance, and he shall dwell in the house of the Lord for six months, with an option to buy. But, the wicked man shall have all kinds of problems. His tongue shall cleave to the roof of his upper palate. And he shall speak like a woman, if you watch him closely. And the wicked man shall be delivered into the hands of his enemy, whether they can pay the delivery charge or not. And, and . . . wait, I have more . . . about the wicked man . . . I shall walk through the valley of the shadow of death . . . in, in fact, now that I think of it, I shall run through the valley of the shadow of death, because you get out of the valley quicker that way. And he that hath clean hands, and a pure heart is okay in my book. But he that fools around with barnyard animals has gotta be watched. I-I thank you. . . .

Love and Death

Aphorisms

The universe is merely a fleeting idea in God's mind—a pretty uncomfortable thought, particularly if you've just made a down payment on a house. . . .

———

Not only is there no God, but try getting a plumber on week-ends.

"My Philosophy"

Inauguration of Master
Simeon Marcus as a member
of the Holy House of Israel,
Leslie's Illustrated News,
April 28, 1877.

My Life Passed Before My Eyes

I was down south once and I was invited to a costume party—
And I figured, what the hell, it's Halloween, I'll go as a ghost.
So I take a sheet off the bed and I throw it over my head. I go
to the party. You have to get the picture. I'm walking down the
street in a Deep Southern town and I have a white sheet over
my head. A car pulls up and three guys with white sheets say,
"Get in." So I figure they're guys going to the party as ghosts. I
get in the car, and I see we're not going to the party, and I tell
them.

They say, "Well, we have to go pick up the Grand
Dragon."

All of a sudden, it hits me. Down South. White sheets.

The Grand Dragon. I put two and two together. I figure, there's a guy going to the party dressed as a dragon.

All of a sudden, a big guy enters the car and I'm sitting there between four Klansmen. Four big-armed men. And the door is locked. I'm petrified. I'm trying to pass, desperately. I'm saying, "You-all" and "Grits." I must have said "Grits" fifty times. They'd ask me a question and I'd say, "Oh, grits. Grits." And next to me is the leader of the Klan—you could tell he's the leader because he's the one wearing contour sheets.

They drive me to an empty field and I gave myself away, because they asked for donations and everybody there gave cash. When they came to me, I said, "I pledge fifty dollars." They knew immediately.

They took my hood off and threw a rope around my neck. They decided to hang me. Suddenly my whole life passed before my eyes. I saw myself as a kid again. In Kansas. Goin' to school. Swimmin' at the swimmin' hole. Fishin'. Fryin' up a mess o' catfish. Goin' down to the general store. Gettin' a piece of gingham for Emmy Lou.

And I realize, it's not my life. They're going to hang me in two minutes and the wrong life is passing before my eyes.

So I spoke to them. I was really eloquent. I said, "Fellas, this country can't survive unless we love one another, regardless of race, creed or color." And they were so moved by my words, not only did they cut me down and let me go, but that night I sold them two thousand dollars' worth of Israel bonds.

Monologue

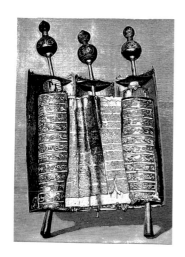

CHAPTER ELEVEN
Death Knocks!

Aren't You Afraid of Dying?

Mickey: I don't understand. I thought you would be happy.
Father: How can we be happy?
Mickey: Well, because I never thought of God in my life.
       Now I'm giving it serious thought.
Father: But Catholicism? Why not your own people?
Mickey: Because I got off on the wrong foot with my own thing,
       you know. But I need a dramatic change in my life.
Father: You're gonna believe in Jesus Christ?
Mickey: I know it sounds funny, but I'm gonna try.
Father: But why? We raised you as a Jew.
Mickey: So? Just 'cause I was born that way . . . you know,
       I'm old enough to make a mature decision.
Father: But why Jesus Christ? Why, for instance, shouldn't
       you become a Buddhist?
Mickey: A Bud—? That's totally alien to me. Look, you're
       getting on in years, right? Aren't you afraid of dying?
Father: Why should I be afraid?
Mickey: Oh! 'Cause you won't exist!
Father: So?
Mickey: That thought doesn't terrify you?
Father: Who thinks of such nonsense? Now I'm alive. When
       I'm dead, I'll be dead.
Mickey: I don't understand. Aren't you frightened?
Father: Of what? I'll be unconscious.
Mickey: Yeah, I know. But never to exist again!
Father: How do you know?
Mickey: Well, it certainly doesn't look promising.
Father: Who knows what'll be? I'll be unconscious or I
       won't. If not, I'll deal with it then. I'm not gonna
       worry now about what's gonna be when I'm uncon-
       scious.
Mickey *(pounding on bathroom door)*: Mom, come out!
Mother *(offscreen in bathroom)*: Of course there's a God, you
       idiot! You don't believe in God?
Mickey: But if there's a God, then why is there so much evil
       in the world? Just on a simplistic level. Why—why
       were there Nazis?
Mother: Tell him, Max!
Father: How the hell do I know why there were Nazis? I
       don't even know how the can opener works.

Hannah and Her Sisters

Tarot card from the Visconti-Sforza, attributed to Bonifacio Bembo, ca. mid 15th century.

Jacques-Louis David, *The Death of Socrates*, 1787.

This Is Your Chance to Die for Truth

Agathon: I told everybody you would die bravely rather than renounce your principles.

Allen: Right, right . . . er, did the concept of "exile" ever come up?

Agathon: They stopped exiling last year. Too much red tape.

Allen: Right, yeah . . . I, er . . . so, er . . . so—what else is new?

Agathon: I ran into Isosceles. He has a great idea for a triangle.

Allen: Right, right . . . look, I'm going to level with you—I don't want to go! I'm too young!

Agathon: But this is your chance to die for truth!

Allen: Don't misunderstand me. I'm all for truth. On the other hand, I have a lunch date in Sparta next week and I'd hate to miss it. It's my turn to buy. You know these Spartans, they fight so easily.

Simmias: Is our wisest philosopher a coward?

Allen: I'm not a coward, and I'm not a hero. I'm somewhere in the middle.

Simmias: A cringing vermin.

Allen: That's approximately the spot.

Agathon: But it was you who proved that death doesn't exist.

Allen: Hey, listen—I've proved a lot of things. That's how I pay my rent. Theories and little observations. A puckish remark now and then. Occasional maxims. It beats picking olives, but let's not get carried away.

Agathon: But you have proved many times that the soul is immortal.

Allen: And it is! On paper. See, that's the thing about philosophy—it's not all that functional once you get out of class.

Simmias: And the external "forms"? You said each thing always did exist and always will exist.

Allen: I was talking mostly about heavy objects. A statue or something. With people it's a lot different.

Agathon: But all that talk about death being the same as sleep.

Allen: Yes, but the difference is that when you're dead and somebody yells, "Everybody up, it's morning," it's very hard to find your slippers.

"My Apology"

Aphorism

It is impossible to experience one's own death objectively and still carry a tune.

"My Philosophy"

Diane Keaton, Kristin Griffith, Mary Beth Hurt, *Interiors.*

Increasing Thoughts of Death

Renata: My impotence set in a year ago. My paralysis. I suddenly found I couldn't bring myself to write anymore. I mean, I shouldn't say "suddenly." Actually, it started happening last winter. Increasing thoughts about death just seemed to come over me. Um . . . these, uh . . . a preoccupation with my own mortality. These feelings of futility in relation to my work. I mean, just what am I striving to create, anyway? I mean, to what end? For what purpose? What goal? I mean . . . do I really care if a handful of my poems are read after I'm gone forever? Is that supposed to be some sort of compensation? I used to think it was. But now, for some reason . . . I can't, I can't seem to . . . I can't . . . seem to shake this . . . this real implication of dying. It's terrifying. The intimacy of it embarrasses me.

Interiors

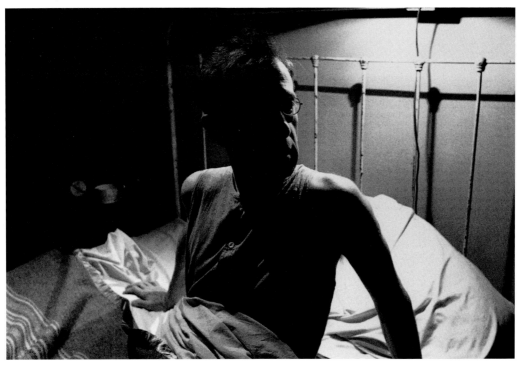

Shadows and Fog

I Just Can't Believe You're Death

Nat: Who are you?

Death: Death. You got a glass of water?

Nat: Death? What do you mean, Death?

Death: What is wrong with you? You see the black costume
and the whitened face?

Nat: Yeah.

Death: Is it Halloween?

Nat: No.

Death: Then I'm Death. Now can I get a glass of water—or a
Fresca?

Nat: If this is some kind of joke—

Death: What kind of joke? You're fifty-seven? Nat
Ackerman? One eighteen Pacific Street? Unless I
blew it—where's that call sheet?

Nat: What do you want with me?

Death: What do I want? What do you think I want?. . .

Nat: Now, wait a minute. I need time. I'm not ready to go.

Death: I'm sorry. I can't help you. I'd like to, but it's the moment.

Nat: How can it be the moment? I just merged with Modiste Originals.

Death: What's the difference, a couple of bucks more or less.

Nat: Sure, what do you care? You guys probably have all your expenses paid.

Death: You want to come along now?

Nat: I'm sorry but I just can't believe you're Death.

Death: Why? What'd you expect—Rock Hudson?

Nat: No, it's not that.

Death: I'm sorry if I disappoint you.

Nat: Now don't get upset. I don't know, I always thought you'd be . . . uh . . . taller.

Death: I'm five-seven. It's average for my weight.

Nat: You look a little like me.

Death: Who should I look like? I'm your Death. . . .

Nat: What'd you mean before when you said this was your first job?

Death: What does it sound like?

Nat: What are you telling me—that nobody ever went before?

Death: Sure they went. But I didn't take them.

Nat: So who did?

Death: Others.

Nat: There's others?

Death: Sure. Each one has his own personal way of going.

Nat: I never knew that.

Death: Why should you know? Who are you?

Nat: What do you mean who am I? Why—I'm nothing?

Death: Not nothing. You're a dress manufacturer. Where do you come to knowledge of the eternal mysteries?

Nat: What are you talking about? I make a beautiful dollar. I sent two kids through college. One is in advertising, the other's married. I got my own home. I drive a Chrysler. My wife has whatever she wants. Maids, mink coat, vacations. Right now she's at the Eden Roc. Fifty dollars a day because she wants to be near her sister. I'm supposed to join her next week, so what do you think I am—some guy off the street?

Death: All right. Don't be so touchy.

Nat: Who's touchy?

Death: How would you like it if I got insulted quickly?

Nat: Did I insult you?

Death: You didn't say you were disappointed in me?

Nat: What do you expect? You want me to throw you a block party?

"Death Knocks"

More Morbid Thoughts

What is it about death that bothers me so much? Probably the hours. Melnick says the soul is immortal and lives on after the body drops away, but if my soul exists without my body I am convinced that all my clothes will be loose-fitting. . . .

"Selections from the Allen Notebooks"

On the Eve of His Execution

Six weeks later, on the eve of his execution, Cloquet sat alone in his cell, still unable to believe the events of the past six months . . . By this time the next day, he would be dead. Cloquet had always thought of Death as something that happened to other people. "I notice it happens to fat people a lot," he told his lawyer. To Cloquet himself, Death seemed to be only another abstraction. Men die, he thought, but does Cloquet die? This question puzzled him, but a few simple line drawings on a pad done by one of the guards set the whole thing clear. There was no evading it. Soon he would no longer exist.

"The Condemned"

Boris: How I got into this predicament, I'll never know. Absolutely incredible. To be executed for a crime I never committed. Of course, isn't all mankind in the same boat? Isn't all mankind ultimately executed for a crime it never committed?

The difference is that all men go eventually . . . but I go six o'clock tomorrow morning. I was supposed to go at five o'clock but I have a smart lawyer. Got leniency.

Love and Death

Awaiting Execution

Alone in a jail cell in Barcelona, a man and his parrot awaited execution. Both were to go before a firing squad the following morning. Both had been found guilty of espionage against the fascists—they had been part of a plot to pass information about troop movements to the underground.

"What time is it?" the man asked nervously.

"Why?" the parrot asked.

"Why? Because we have a certain interest in the time, don't you think?"

"All right, all right, don't get upset. Pass me that piece of orange, will you?"

"How can you eat at a moment like this?" the man said.

"Look, we got a bad break. What do you want me to do? Give up meals?"

"Break, nothing. If Arroyo had blown up the bridge instead of running away. . . ."

"Right, like I said, a bad break. Now will you pass me a piece of orange and stop pacing, you're making me dizzy."

"I don't want to die," the man said, pounding the wall.

"What do you mean, 'die'?" the parrot asked. "What is 'die'?"

"What do you mean, what is 'die'? What the hell is wrong with you?"

"I'm a parrot."

"So you don't know what it means to die? To be dead?"

"Correct me if I'm wrong," the bird ventured, "eyes closed, on your back, difficulty swallowing?"

"That's close enough," the man said, exasperated.

"It doesn't sound too bad," the parrot answered.

The man tried to explain. "Jose, it means everything is over. No more sunshine, no more music, no more laughter."

"Yeah . . . ?" The parrot, clearly bewildered, tried to grasp this.

"Yeah. So what are you looking at me like that for? Does that sound good?"

"I don't know," the parrot said.

"Y'know, not only are you a parrot, but I'll bet even among your own you're in the bottom ten percent."

"Yeah? Well, too bad. At least I'm not a whiner."

"Supposing the priests are right?" the man wondered.

"Meaning what?"

"Meaning, what if there's a heaven and a hell or something like that? What if it turns out I'm damned for all eternity? Consigned to roast in a fiery furnace for countless eons?"

"Roast? Roast what?" the parrot asked.

"Oh Jesus," the man sighed exasperatedly.

"Besides, what are you so guilty about?" the parrot asked. "You'd think you carried on."

"Oh, and I suppose you've led a perfectly clean life?" the man argued.

"Look, pal, how many times do I have to explain to you? I'm a bird. To me, a big night is to swing back and forth on my perch."

"All I know is, I don't want to die." The man was sweating now.

"And all I know is I've got to have a piece of orange because I'm getting a headache."

The two sat in silence for a while. The man couldn't eat. He tried to tell himself that at least he was dying for a good cause, but it was little comfort. He felt sorry for the parrot.

"Why'd you get into this war?" he asked the bird.

"The underground was looking for some way they could get information out without appearing suspicious," said the parrot. "They were going to use a mynah bird, but they're so unreliable. Although I once knew one who could type a few letters."

"Did you always hate the fascists?" the man asked.

"Hate the fascists? Rodriguez, I don't even know what the fascists are! The sum total of my political orientation consists of: Don't go near cats. O.K.?"

"Well, why didn't you refuse if you had no political convictions?"

"I'm somebody's pet. Since when do I have a say in things?"

"You couldn't say no?"

"You got to be kidding. I sit on a swing in a cage and stare out into space. You think if the family makes a decision they consult me? That's really funny! I can see it now: 'Darling, I've decided to sell the house and move to London, let's check with the parrot and get his feelings on it.' " The parrot was hysterical now.

Rodriguez was becoming desperate. "You can save us, you know that."

"Let's not get into that again," the parrot said wearily.

"But if you just tell them the information they want to know. You're the only one who has the information."

"I was ordered never to inform."

"It's not informing, Jose. Our lives are at stake."

"I was told not to repeat it," the parrot said mechanically.

"But all they want to know are some dates. And they'll probably let us go."

"I can't do it."

"Damn you," the man said, exploding. "I'm going to pull every feather in your tail out." Rodriguez chased the fluttering bird around the tiny cell.

"Not only won't I tell, but when we get back to the underground, I'm going to say you wanted me to," the parrot shrieked.

"You idiot. You jerk. We're not getting back to the underground. That's the point. Only you can save us. Can you understand what life is about? What dying means? The preciousness of time? What a stupid species."

"I'm not following," the parrot said, blithely munching on his orange slice.

"Why couldn't I be here with a dog?" the man sighed. "At least they're loyal."

"Sure they're loyal," the parrot said, "but can they talk?"

"What's the use?" Rodriguez said, and sat down, burying his head in his hands.

Five minutes before dawn a priest came to the cell and asked if either of the prisoners would like the last rites.

"I'm an atheist," the man said.

"Last rites?" the parrot said. "I don't get it."

"Don't even start a conversation with him, Father," the man said, "because you'll wind up behind the eight ball."

The matter was closed and presently the two were taken out to the yard. The man was blindfolded and he and the parrot were stood against a wall.

"Why are you wearing that silly cloth over your eyes?" the parrot asked as the firing squad raised their rifles.

"Look, don't talk to me. We got nothing in common. You belong to a species that will never distinguish itself. You have no sensitivity or grasp of the big questions. I'm deeper, more profound, and in every way your moral, spiritual and intellectual superior. I die like a man, you like a creature."

Then, just before the triggers were squeezed, the parrot

flew up and safely away. The shots rang out, executing the man.

"What you say may be so," the parrot yelled to the crumpled heap below, "but at least I can fly, which can come in handy under certain circumstances."

"The Penalty"

Certain Tribes in Borneo

O. F. Krumgold has written a brilliant paper about certain tribes in Borneo that do not have a word for "no" in their language and consequently turn down requests by nodding their heads and saying "I'll get back to you." This corroborates his earlier theories that the urge to be liked at any cost is not socially adaptive but genetic, much the same as the ability to sit through operetta.

"By Destiny Denied"

Dying Doesn't Make You Thirsty

John: Bring him some water.
Kleinman: What do I need water for?
John: I assumed you were thirsty.
Kleinman: Dying doesn't make you thirsty. Unless you get stabbed after eating herring.
John: Are you afraid of dying?
Kleinman: It's not that I'm afraid of dying. I just don't want to be there when it happens.

Death (A Play)

Sandor Needleman Is Dead

It has been four weeks and it is still hard for me to believe Sandor Needleman is dead. I was present at the cremation and at his son's request, brought the marshmallows, but few of us could think of anything but our pain.

Needleman was constantly obsessing over his funeral plans and once told me, "I much prefer cremation to burial in the earth, and both to a weekend with Mrs. Needleman."

"Remembering Needleman"

Being Dead

Man: Dead. I've been dead. During the war. Wounded. There I lay on the operating table. Surgeons sweating to save my life. Suddenly they lost me—pulse stopped. It was all over. One of 'em, I'm told, had the presence of mind to massage my heart. Then it began beating again, so I lived, but for a tiny moment there, I was officially dead. . . . According to science, too—dead . . . but that was a long time ago. . . .

Kleinman: So how was it? . . . Being dead. Did you see anything?

Man: No. It was just . . . nothing.

Kleinman: You don't remember any afterlife?

Man: No.

Kleinman: My name didn't come up?

Man: There was nothing. There is nothing after, Kleinman. Nothing.

Death (A Play)

Not Dying

I don't want to achieve immortality through my work, I want to achieve it through not dying.

Interview

Listen, I Don't Know from Suicide

Cliff: The guy was not sick at all. And he left a note. He left a simple note that said, "I've gone out the window." And this is a major intellectual, and he leaves this note. "I've gone out the window." I mean, what the hell does that mean? This guy was a role model. You'd think he'd leave a decent note.

Halley: Well, did he have any family or anything?

Cliff: No, 'cause they were all killed in the war. That's what's so strange about this. He'd seen the worst side of life. His whole life he was always affirmative. He always said yes to life. Yes, yes. Now, today, he says no. . . . Listen, I don't know from suicide. When I grew up in Brooklyn, nobody committed suicide. Everybody was too unhappy.

Crimes and Misdemeanors

Annie Hall

Book of the Dead of Khensmose, Agyptische Kunst, (21. Dynastie, 11.-10. JH.V.CHR.)

They Buried the Wrong Man

New Orleans: A jazz band stands in the rain at a cemetery playing mournful hymns as a body is lowered into the earth. Now they strike up a spirited march and begin the parade back to town. Halfway there, someone realizes they have buried the wrong man. What's more, they weren't even close. The person they buried was not dead, or even sick; in fact, he was yodeling at the time. They return to the cemetery and exhume the poor man, who threatens to sue, although they promise to let him have his suit cleaned and send them the bill. Meanwhile, no one knows which person is actually dead. The band continues to play while each of the onlookers is buried in turn, on the theory that the deceased will go down the smoothest. Soon it becomes apparent that no one has died, and now it is too late to get a body, because of the holiday rush.

"Reminiscences: Places and People"

Considering I'm Dead

Eddie: God, you're even more beautiful now. It's been almost
twenty years. Tell me I don't look so bad considering
I'm dead.

Alice: Oh no, considering you're dead, you look great.

Alice

Sonja: You were my one great love!

Boris: Oh, thank you very much. I appreciate that, now if
you'll excuse me, I'm dead.

Sonja: What's it like?

Boris: What's it like? Ah . . . you know the chicken at
Tresky's restaurant?

Sonja: Yeah.

Boris: It's worse.

Love and Death

Do You Believe in Reincarnation?

Doctor: Kleinman, do you believe in reincarnation?

Kleinman: What's that?

Doctor: Reincarnation—that a person comes back to life
again as something else.

Kleinman: Like what?

Doctor: Er . . . uh . . . another living thing. . . .

Kleinman: What do you mean? Like an animal?

Doctor: Yes.

Kleinman: You mean like you may live again as a frog?

Doctor: Forget it, Kleinman, I didn't say anything.

Kleinman: Listen, anything's possible, but it's hard to imagine if a man is president of a big corporation in this
life, that he'll wind up a chipmunk.

Death (A Play)

An Unseen World

There is no question that there is an unseen world. The problem is, how far is it from midtown and how late is it open? Unexplainable events occur constantly. One man will see spirits. Another will hear voices. A third will wake up and find himself running in the Preakness. How many of us have not at one time or another felt an ice-cold hand on the back of our neck while we were home alone? (Not me, thank God, but some have.) What is behind these experiences? Or in front of them, for that matter? Is it true that some men can foresee the future or communicate with ghosts? And after death is it still possible to take showers?

"Examining Psychic Phenomena"

This Hollow Charade

No use, Cloquet reflected. I will have to meet my fate alone. There is no God. There is no purpose in life. Nothing lasts. Even the works of the great Shakespeare will disappear when the universe burns out—not such a terrible thought, of course, when it comes to a play like *Titus Andronicus,* but what about the others? No wonder some people commit suicide! Why not end this absurdity? Why go through with this hollow charade called life? Why, except that somewhere within us a voice says, "Live." Always, from some inner region, we hear the command, "Keep living!" Cloquet recognized the voice; it was his insurance salesman. Naturally, he thought—Fishbein doesn't want to pay off.

"The Condemned"

"Oedipus Wrecks," *New York Stories*

An Interesting Seance Experience

We attended the home of Madame Reynaud, the noted medium, where we were all told to sit around the table and join hands. The lights were turned out, and Madame Reynaud attempted to contact Mrs. Marple's husband, who had died at the opera when his beard caught fire. The following is an exact transcript:

Mrs. Marple: What do you see?
Medium: I see a man with blue eyes and a pinwheel hat.
Mrs. Marple: That's my husband!
Medium: His name is . . . Robert. No . . . Richard. . . .
Mrs. Marple: Quincy.
Medium: Quincy! Yes, that's it!
Mrs. Marple: What else about him?
Medium: He is bald but usually keeps some leaves of lettuce
        on his head so nobody will notice.
Mrs. Marple: Yes! Exactly!

Medium: For some reason, he has an object . . . a loin of pork.

Mrs. Marple: My anniversary present to him! Can you make him speak?

Medium: Speak, spirit, speak.

Quincy: Claire, this is Quincy.

Mrs. Marple: Oh, Quincy! Quincy!

Quincy: How long do you keep the chicken in when trying to broil it?

Mrs. Marple: That voice! It's him!

Medium: Quincy, are they treating you okay?

Quincy: Not bad, except that it takes four days to get your cleaning back.

Mrs. Marple: Quincy, do you miss me?

Quincy: Huh? Oh, er, sure. Sure, kid. I got to be going. . . .

Medium: I'm losing him. He's fading. . . .

I found this seance to pass the most stringent tests of credulity, with the minor exception of a phonograph, which was found under Madame Reynaud's dress.

There is no doubt that certain events recorded at seances are genuine. . . . But contacting the dead is at best difficult, since most deceased are reluctant to speak up, and those that do seem to hem and haw before getting to the point. The author has actually seen a table rise, and Dr. Joshua Fleagle, of Harvard, attended a seance in which a table not only rose but excused itself and went upstairs to sleep.

"Examining Psychic Phenomena"

I grew weary and contemplated suicide. I held a pistol to my head, but at the last moment lost my nerve and fired in the air. The bullet passed through my ceiling, causing Mrs. Fitelson in the apartment overhead to leap straight upward onto her bookshelf and remain perched there throughout the High Holidays.

"The Lunatic's Tale"

Did He Suffer Much?

I once had a pain in the chestal area. I was sure it was heart-burn because at that time I was married and my wife was cooking her Nazi recipe. Chicken Himmler.

I didn't want to pay twenty-five bucks to have it reaf-firmed by some medic that I had heartburn but I was worried because it was in the chestal area. Then it turns out my friend Eggs Benedict has a pain in his chestal area in the exact same spot. I figured if I could get Eggs to go to the doctor, I could figure out what was wrong with me at no charge.

So I con Eggs. He goes. Turns out he's got heartburn. Costs him twenty-five dollars. And I feel great because I beat the medic out of twenty-five big ones.

Call up Eggs two days later. He died.

I check into a hospital immediately. Have a battery of tests drawn. X-rays. Turns out I got heartburn. Costs me one hundred and ten dollars.

Now I'm furious. I run into Egg's mother and I say, "Did he suffer much?"

And she said, "No, it was quick. Car hit him and that was it."

Monologue

An Afterlife

Once again I tried committing suicide—this time by wetting my nose and inserting it into the light socket. Unfortunately, there was a short in the wiring, and I merely caromed off the icebox. Still obsessed by thoughts of death, I brood constant-ly. I keep wondering if there is an afterlife, and if there is will they be able to break a twenty?

"Selections from the Allen Notebooks"

I don't believe in an afterlife, although I am bringing a change of underwear.

"Conversations with Helmholtz"

You Guys Believe in Reincarnation

Krishna leader: What makes you interested in becoming a
      Hare Krishna?
Mickey: Well, I'm not saying that I want to join or anything,
      but . . . but I know you guys believe in reincarnation,
      you know, so it interests me.
Krishna leader: Yeah, well, what's your religion?
Mickey: Well, I was born Jewish, you know, but last winter I
      tried to become a Catholic and . . . it didn't work for
      me. I studied and I tried and I gave it everything but,
      you know, Catholicism for me was die now, pay later,
      you know. And I just couldn't get with it. And I, and
      I, wanted to, you know. . . .
Krishna leader: You're afraid of dying?
Mickey: Well . . . yeah, naturally. Aren't you? Let me ask
      you, reincarnation, does that mean my soul would
      pass to another human being, or would I come back
      as a moose or an aardvark or something?
Krishna leader: Take our literature, read it over and think
      about it. . . .
Mickey *(voice over):* Who are you kidding? You're gonna
      become a Krishna? You're gonna shave your head
      and put on robes and dance around at airports? You'll
      look like Jerry Lewis. Oh, God, I'm so depressed.

Hannah and Her Sisters

Immortality

Vivian: Sandy Bates's works will live on after him.
Sandy: Yeah, but what good is it if I can't pinch any women
      or hear any music?

Stardust Memories

Someone once asked me if my dream was to live on in the
hearts of my people, and I said I would like to live on in my
apartment. And that's really what I would prefer.

Rolling Stone interview

CHAPTER TWELVE

Things That Make Life Worth Living

Charlotte Rampling and Woody Allen, *Stardust Memories*.

And for One Brief Moment

Sandy: When you're dying, uh, life suddenly really does
become very authentic. And . . . and, uh, something . . . I was
reaching for something to give my life meaning and . . . and a
memory flashed through my mind. It was one of those great
spring days. It was Sunday, and you knew summer would be
coming soon. I remember, that morning Dorrie and I had gone
for a walk in the park. We came back to the apartment. We
were just sort of sitting around. And . . . I put on a record of
Louis Armstrong, which is music I grew up loving. It was
very, very pretty, and . . . I happened to glance over, and I saw
Dorrie sitting there. And I remember thinking to myself how
terrific she was, and how much I loved her. And, I don't know,
I guess it was the combination of everything . . . the sound of
that music, and the breeze and, how beautiful Dorrie looked
to me. And for one brief moment, everything just seemed to
come together perfectly, and I felt happy. Almost indestruc-
tible, in a way.

Stardust Memories

Radio Days

I Never Forgot That New Year's Eve

Joe: I never forgot that New Year's Eve when Aunt Bea awakened me to watch 1944 come in. I've never forgotten any of those people or any of the voices we would hear on the radio. Though the truth is, with the passing of each New Year's Eve those voices do seem to grow dimmer and dimmer.

Radio Days

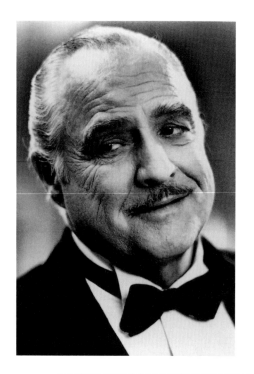

Why Is Life Worth Living?

Ike: An idea for a short story . . . about, um, people in Manhattan who, uh, who are constantly creating these real, uh, unnecessary neurotic problems for themselves 'cause it keeps them from dealing with, uh, more unsolvable, terrifying problems about, uh, the universe . . . well, it has to be optimistic. Well, all right, why is life worth living? That's a very good question.

Um. Well, there are certain things I guess that make it worthwhile. Uh, like what? Okay, for me . . . oh, I would say . . . what, Groucho Marx, to name one thing . . . uh, Willie Mays, and the second movement of the Jupiter Symphony, and, um, Louis Armstrong's recording of "Potatohead Blues" . . . um, Swedish movies, naturally, Sentimental Education by Flaubert . . . um, Marlon Brando, Frank Sinatra . . . um, those incredible apples and pears by Cézanne . . . uh, the crabs at Sam Wo's . . . uh, Tracy's face. . . .

Manhattan

Above: Willie Mays

Left: Groucho Marx

OPPOSITE PAGE
Top left: Marlon Brando
Top right: Louis Armstrong
Bottom: Paul Cézanne,
The Basket of Apples, c. 1895.

265

Have I Learned Anything About Life?

Boris: The question is, have I learned anything about life? Only that, only that human beings are divided into mind and body. The mind embraces all the nobler aspirations, like, poetry, and philosophy, but, the body has all the fun.

The important thing, I think, is not to be bitter. You know, if it turns out that there is a God, I don't think He's evil. I think that the worst that you could say about Him, is that basically, He's an underachiever.

After all, you know, there are worse things than death. I mean, if you've, if you've ever spent an evening with an insurance salesman, you know exactly what I mean. The key here, I think, is to not think of death as an end, but, think of it more as a very effective way of cutting down on your expenses.

Regarding love, you know, what can I say? It's not the, the quantity of your sexual relations that count, it's the quality. On the other hand, if the quantity drops below once every eight months, I would definitely look into it. Well, that's about it.

Love and Death

The Secret's Not Being You

Bogart: That was great. You've really developed yourself a little style.

Allen: Yeah. I do have a certain amount of style, don't I?

Bogart: Well, I guess you won't be needing me any more. There's nothing I can tell you now that you don't already know.

Allen: I guess that's so. I guess the secret's not being you— it's being me. True, you're not too tall and kinda ugly but—what the hell—I'm short enough and ugly enough to succeed on my own.

Play It Again, Sam

Humphrey Bogart, *To Have and Have Not*, 1945.

Which Road Her Life Will Take

Dr. Yang: Mrs. Tate had illusion of happiness. Upon closer observation, not very honest husband, not very honest with self. . . . I think Mrs. Tate has better idea of who she is then before she came to Dr. Yang. Who her friends are or are not. Who is husband, lover, sister,

Mia Farrow and Woody Allen on the set of *Shadows and Fog*.

mother. What are her needs, her limits, her gifts. What are her innermost feelings. May not know all answers but has better idea. No?

Alice: Yes, yes, it's true.

Dr. Yang: Now must decide which road her life will take.

Alice

How I Feel About Life

Alvy: There's this old joke. Uh, two elderly women are at a Catskills mountain resort, and one of 'em says: "Boy, the food at this place is really terrible." The other one says, "Yeah, I know, and such small portions." Well, that's essentially how I feel about life. Full of loneliness and misery and suffering and unhappiness, and it's all over much too quickly.

The—the other important joke for me is one that's, uh, usually attributed to Groucho Marx, but I think it appears originally in Freud's *Wit and Its Relation to the Unconscious*. And it goes like this—I'm paraphrasing: Uh . . . "I would never wanna belong to any club that would have someone like me for a member." That's the key joke of my adult life in terms of my relationships with women.

You know, lately the strangest things have been going through my mind, 'cause I turned forty, and I guess I'm going through a life crisis or something, I don't know. I . . . and I'm not worried about aging. I'm not one of those characters, you know. Although I'm balding slightly on top, that's about the worst you can say about me.

I . . . I think I'm gonna get better as I get older, you know? I think I'm gonna be the—the balding virile type, you know, as opposed to say the, uh, distinguished gray, for instance, you know? 'Less I'm neither of those two. Unless I'm one of those guys with saliva dribbling out of his mouth who wanders into a cafeteria with a shopping bag screaming about socialism.

Annie Hall

The Secret of Life

The Emperor Ho Sin had a dream in which he beheld a palace greater than his for half the rent. Stepping through the portals of the edifice, Ho Sin suddenly found that his body became young again, although his head remained somewhere between sixty-five and seventy. Opening a door, he found another door, which led to another; soon he realized he had entered a hundred doors and was now out in the backyard.

Just when Ho Sin was on the verge of despair, a nightingale perched on his shoulder and sang the most beautiful

A Memory

And I wondered if a memory is something you have or something you've lost. . . .

Another Woman

Pushcart Market, New York City, 1945.

One Great Regret

His one great regret in life is that he is not someone else.

Getting Even

Summing Up

In summing up, it is clear the future holds great opportunities. It also holds pitfalls. The trick is to avoid the pitfalls, seize the opportunities and get back home by six o'clock.

"My Speech to the Graduates"

In summing up, I wish I had some kind of affirmative message to leave you with. I don't.
    Would you take two negative messages?

Monologue

Hannah and Her Sisters

Sources

Unpublished Screenplays

This book contains excerpts from the twenty-six screenplays written by Woody Allen. Sixteen of these screenplays have never been published, and excerpts were taken from the original scripts on file with Rollins and Joffe, Inc. (Jack Rollins and Charles Joffe have been Woody Allen's personal managers since the mid-1960s and have produced all of his movies.) In some cases, Rollins and Joffe supplied several drafts of original scripts. Except as otherwise specified in the Notes, excerpts from the following movies are quoted directly from Woody Allen's original screenplays:

What's New Pussycat? (Famous Artists, 1965)
What's Up, Tiger Lily? (American International Pictures, 1966. Originally produced and released in Japan as *Kagi No Kagi* [Key of Keys] in 1964.)
Take the Money and Run (Palomar Pictures, 1969), co-written by Mickey Rose.
Bananas (United Artists, 1971), co-written by Mickey Rose.
Everything You Always Wanted to Know About Sex* (*But Were Afraid to Ask) (United Artists, 1972)
Sleeper (United Artists, 1973), co-written by Marshall Brickman.
Love and Death (United Artists, 1975)
Midsummer Night's Sex Comedy (Orion Pictures, 1982)

Radio Days (Orion Pictures, 1987)
September (Orion Pictures, 1987)
Another Woman (Orion Pictures, 1988)
"Oedipus Wrecks" from *New York Stories* (Touchstone Pictures, 1989)
Crimes and Misdemeanors (Orion Pictures, 1990)
Alice (Orion Pictures, 1990)
Shadows and Fog (Orion Pictures, 1992)
Husbands and Wives (Orion Pictures, 1992)

Published Screenplays

Don't Drink the Water (Random House, 1967)
Play It Again, Sam (Random House, 1969)
Woody Allen's Play It Again, Sam (Grosset and Dunlap, 1972)
Four Films of Woody Allen (Random House, 1982), which includes: *Annie Hall* (United Artists, 1977), co-written by Marshall Brickman; *Interiors* (United Artists, 1978); *Manhattan* (United Artists, 1979), co-written by Marshall Brickman; and *Stardust Memories* (United Artists, 1980)
Hannah and Her Sisters (Random House, 1987)
Three Films of Woody Allen (Vintage Books, 1987), which includes: *Zelig* (Orion Pictures, 1983); *Broadway Danny Rose* (Orion Pictures, 1984); and *The Purple Rose of Cairo* (Orion Pictures, 1985)

Books

Woody Allen is the author of more than sixty essays, most of which were first published in *The New Yorker*, *Kenyon Review*, *The New Republic*, and *Playboy* or *Life* magazines, and then collected in the following anthologies:

Getting Even (Random House, 1971; Vintage Books, 1978)
Without Feathers (Random House, 1975; Warners Books, 1976)
Side Effects (Random House, 1975; Ballantine Books, 1981)
The Complete Prose of Woody Allen: Without Feathers, Getting Even and Side Effects (Wings Books/Random House, 1991)

Record Albums

Woody Allen's stand-up monologues have never been previously published in book form. For the numerous excerpts quoted in this book, monologues were transcribed from the following records, also made available from Rollins and Joffe, Inc.:

Woody Allen (Colpix, 1964)
Woody Allen, Volume 2 (Colpix, 1965)
The Third Woody Allen Album (Capitol, 1968)
Woody Allen: The Nightclub Years, 1964–1968 (United Artists, 1976), and *Woody Allen Standup Comic, 1964–1968* (Casablanca Records, 1978), two compilation albums of previously recorded monologues.

Notes

Introduction: You Should Know That About Me

8: "Woody Allen's First Recorded Monologue" was recorded live at Mr. Kelly's in Chicago, March 1964, and released as "Private Life" on *Woody Allen* and both compilation albums.

Chapter One: My Parents' Values: God and Carpeting

15: "Reminiscences: Places and People" first appeared in *The New Yorker*, December 29, 1975, and was reprinted in *Side Effects*.

16: "Coney Island" was recorded live at the Shadows in Washington, D.C., April 1965, and released as "Unhappy Childhood" on *Woody Allen, Volume 2*. An edited version was also released on both compilation albums.

18: "The Sensitive Kid" was recorded at Mr. Kelly's in Chicago, March 1964, and appeared as "Brooklyn" on *Woody Allen* and both compilation albums.

20: "No Kaddish for Weinstein" first appeared in *The New Yorker*, March 3, 1975, and was reprinted in *Without Feathers*.

24: "Throw the Kid Out" was recorded live at the Shadows in Washington, D.C., April 1965, and released as "The Kidnapping" on *Woody Allen, Volume 2* and both compilation albums.

26: Woody Allen, "How Bogart Made Me the Superb Lover I Am Today," *Life* magazine, March 21, 1969.

27: "Confessions of a Burglar" first appeared in *The New Yorker*, October 18, 1976, and was reprinted in *Side Effects*. "The Irish Genius" first appeared in *The New Republic*, February 22, 1975, and was reprinted in *Without Feathers*. "WOODY ALLEN (Alan Felix) . . ." appeared as a biography in the *Playbill* magazine for the opening of *Play It Again, Sam*, which was performed on stage at the Broadhurst Theater in New York City. The play was written by and starred Woody Allen and ran from February 12, 1969 to March 14, 1970. It was later made into a movie starring Woody Allen and Diane Keaton.

28: "The Condemned" first appeared in *The New Yorker*, November 21, 1977, and was reprinted in *Side Effects*.

29: "Lovborg's Women Considered" first appeared in *The New Yorker*, October 28, 1974, and was reprinted in *Without Feathers*.

30: "My Mother Went Crazy with Name Tags" was included in the original script of *What's New Pussycat?* but was cut from the film. "The Heart of the Old World" monologue was recorded live at Mr. Kelly's in Chicago, March 1964, and released as "NYU" on *Woody Allen*. A severely cut and edited version is included on both compilation albums.

32: "Confessions of a Burglar," see note for page 27. "Fine Times: An Oral Memoir" first appeared in *The New Yorker*, March 17, 1975, and was reprinted in *Without Feathers*.

33: "Selections from the Allen Notebooks" first appeared in *The New Yorker*, November 5, 1973, and was reprinted in *Without Feathers*. "Retribution" first appeared in *Kenyon Review*, Summer 1980, and was reprinted in *Side Effects*.

35: "No Kaddish for Weinstein," see note for page 20.

36: "My Grandfather Was a Very Insignificant Man" was recorded live at Mr. Kelly's in Chicago, March 1964, and released as "My Grandfather" on *Woody Allen* and both compilation albums.

39: A dramatic play written for the stage, *The Floating Lightbulb* opened on Monday, April 27, 1981, at the Vivian Beaumont Theater in New York City. The play was published in book form in 1982 by Random House, but is now out of print.

41: "If the Impressionists Had Been Dentists" first appeared in *Without Feathers*.

Chapter Two: An Unsentimental Education

45: "Military School" is part of a much longer monologue called "A Love Story," which was recorded live at Mr. Kelly's in Chicago in March 1964, and released on *Woody Allen* and both compilation albums.

50: Jack Kroll, "Woody," *Newsweek*, April 24, 1978.

52: "Spring Bulletin" first appeared in *The New Yorker*, April 29, 1967, and was reprinted in *Getting Even*. "A History of Hygiene Major" is part of a much longer monologue entitled "Second Marriage," which was recorded live at Eugene's in San Francisco, August 1968, and released on *The Third Woody Allen Album*. A cut and edited version also appears on both compilation albums.

54: "Mr. Big" first appeared in *Getting Even*. "Deep Philosophical Arguments" was part of a much longer monologue recorded live at Mr. Kelly's in Chicago in March 1964, and released as "NYU" on *Woody Allen* and, in a severely cut and edited version, on both compilation albums.

Chapter Three: Intellectuals Only Kill Their Own

59: "Fabulous Tales and Mythical Beasts" first appeared in *The New Republic*, November 30, 1974, and was reprinted in *Without Feathers*.

61: "The Metterling Lists" first appeared in *The New Yorker*, May 10, 1969, and was reprinted in *Getting Even*. "Woody, the Would-Be Critic," was published in *The New York Times*, Sunday, May 2, 1971. The byline read: "By Woody Allen, star and director of *Bananas*, now at the Coronet."

62: "The UFO Menace" first appeared in *The New Yorker*, June 13, 1977, and was reprinted in *Side Effects*. "So that's how a genius seduces a woman . . ." appeared in the original screen-

play of *A Midsummer Night's Sex Comedy* but was cut from the final edit of film.

63: "Selections from the Allen Notebooks," see note for page 33.

64: "My Apology" was first published in *Side Effects*. "The Irish Genius" first appeared in *The New Republic*, February 22, 1975, and was reprinted in *Without Feathers*. "Remembering Needleman" first appeared in *The New Republic* (as "At the Cremation: Remembering Needleman"), July 24, 1976, and was reprinted as "Remembering Needleman" in *Side Effects*.

65: "Examining Psychic Phenomena" first appeared in *The New Yorker*, October 7, 1972, and was reprinted in *Without Feathers*.

Chapter Four: New York vs. Los Angeles

71: "No Kaddish for Weinstein," see note for page 20. Written in 1975, *God (A Play)* was first published in *Without Feathers*. A performance edition of the short play, entitled *God*, was published by Samuel French in 1975.

73: "The Fools in Hollywood" was excerpted from the original first draft of *Take the Money and Run*. A slightly altered version of this monologue was included in the film. "In Downtown Los Angeles" was recorded live at Eugene's in San Francisco, August 1968, and released as "Mechanical Objects" on *The Third Woody Allen Album*. A cut and edited version appears on both compilation albums.

75: Sol Weinstein, "*Playboy* Interview: Woody Allen,"

Playboy, May 1967. "The Whore of Mensa" first appeared in *The New Yorker*, December 16, 1974, and was reprinted in *Without Feathers*.

78: "Running Down Fifth Avenue," part of "The Great Renaldo" monologue, was recorded live at Eugene's in San Francisco, in August 1968 and released on *The Third Woody Allen Album* and both compilation albums.

80: William Geist, "The *Rolling Stone* Interview: Woody Allen," *Rolling Stone* #497, April 9, 1987.

Chapter Five: Love: The Good Sentimental

82: "Selections from the Allen Notebooks," see note on page 33.

84: "The Early Essays" (including "On Seeing a Tree in Summer," "On Youth and Age," "On Frugality," "On Love," and "On Tripping Through a Copse and Picking Violets") first appeared in *The New Yorker*, January 20, 1973, and was reprinted in *Without Feathers*.

85: "The Lunatic's Tale" first appeared in *The New Republic*, April 23, 1977, and was reprinted in *Side Effects*.

86: "I Knew I Was in Love," a monologue done in voice-over in *Take the Money and Run*, was not part of the original screenplay. This monologue was transcribed from a tape of the film.

92: "The Scrolls" first appeared in *The New Republic*, August 31, 1974, and was reprinted in *Without Feathers*.

95: "A Twenties Memory" was first published in *Getting Even* and later reprinted in *The Saturday Evening Post*, July 1978. Also see note for page 152.

96: *God* (A Play), see note for page 71. "Something Seductive About Me" was recorded live at Eugene's in San Francisco, in August 1968, and released as "Las Vegas" on *The Third Woody Allen Album* and, slightly trimmed, as "Vegas" on the compilation albums.

98: "They Threw Me Out of Masters and Johnson" was transcribed from a tape of *Everything You Always Wanted to Know About Sex . . .* and was not part of the original screenplay of the movie.

99: "Sex and Love" was transcribed from a tape of *A Midsummer Night's Sex Comedy* and appeared as part of a much longer scene in the original screenplay of the movie. "The Condemned," see note for page 28.

101: "The Lunatic's Tale," see note for page 85. "A Bad History with Blind Dates" is part of a much longer monologue called "Second Marriage," which was recorded live at Eugene's in San Francisco, August 1968, and released on *The Third Woody Allen Album* and both compilation albums.

104: "She Was Violated" is part of a much longer monologue called "Second Marriage," which was recorded live at Eugene's in San Francisco, August 1968, and released on *The Third Woody Allen Album* and both compilation albums. "The Lunatic's Tale," see note for page 85.

109: "The Lunatic's Tale," see note for page 85. "Retribution" first appeared in *Kenyon Review*, Summer 1980, and was reprinted in *Side Effects*.

118: "I Had a Rough Marriage" was recorded live at Mr. Kelly's in Chicago, in March 1964, and released as "My Marriage" on *Woody Allen* and, in an edited form, on both compilation albums.

121: "No Kaddish for Weinstein," see note for page 20.

Chapter Six: These Modern Analysts!

126: "No Kaddish for Weinstein," see note for page 20.

128: "The Irish Genius," see note for page 27.

129: "I'm a Doctor of the Mind" does not appear in either the first or second drafts of the screenplay for *What's New Pussycat?*, and was transcribed from a tape of the movie.

131: "I Was Going to Kill Myself" was part of a much longer monologue called "Second Marriage," which was recorded live at Eugene's in San Francisco, August 1968, and released on *The Third Woody Allen Album*. A cut and edited version also appears on both compilation albums.

135: "Selections from the Allen Notebooks," see note for page 33.

136: "The UFO Menace," see note for page 62.

139: "Nefarious Times We Live In" first appeared in *The New Republic*, November 22, 1975,

and was reprinted in *Side Effects*. "You'll Like This Group Analysis" was transcribed from a tape of *What's New Pussycat?*, and does not appear in this form on either the first or second drafts of the original screenplay.

142: "Conversations with Helmholtz" first appeared in *Getting Even*.

143: "The Kugelmass Episode" first appeared in *The New Yorker*, May 2, 1977, and was reprinted in *Side Effects*.

Chapter Seven: Work, Art and Funnier Jokes

147: "The First Time I Ever Acted" was recorded live at the Shadows, in Washington, D.C., in April 1965, and released as "What's New Pussycat?" on *Woody Allen, Volume 2*. The monologue was cut, edited and renamed "European Trip" for the two compilation albums.

149: *The Floating Lightbulb*, see note for page 39.

152: "The Lost Generation" was recorded live at the Shadows in Washington, D.C., April 1965, and released on *Woody Allen, Volume 2* and both compilation albums. The same material, written in essay form as "A Twenties Memory," was published in *Getting Even* and later reprinted in *The Saturday Evening Post*, July 1978.

155: "Reminiscences: Places and People," see note for page 15.

156: "Woody, the Would-Be Critic," see note for page 61.

158: "The UFO Menace," see note for page 62. "I Wrote a

Science Fiction Film" was recorded live at the Shadows in Washington, D.C., April 1965, and released as "Science Fiction Movie" on *Woody Allen, Volume 2*, and as "The Science Fiction Film" on both compilation albums.

160: "Lovborg's Women Considered," see note for page 29. "A Giant Step for Mankind" first appeared in *The New Yorker*, June 9, 1980, and was later reprinted in *Side Effects*.

163: "Yes, But Can the Steam Engine Do This?" first appeared in *The New Yorker*, October 6, 1966, and was reprinted in *Getting Even*.

164: "The Discovery and Use of the Fake Ink Blot" first appeared in *Playboy*, August 1966, and was reprinted in *Getting Even*. "By Destiny Denied" first appeared in *The New Yorker*, February 23, 1976, and was reprinted in *Side Effects*.

165: "We're on a Waiting List," was transcribed from a tape of *What's Up, Tiger Lily?* as the written screenplay of the film no longer exists.

168: "I Got a Job on Madison Avenue" is part of a much longer monologue called "Love Story," which was recorded live at Mr. Kelly's in Chicago, March 1964, and released on *Woody Allen*. An edited version appears on both compilation albums. "Nice job" was not included on either the first or second drafts of the screenplay for *What's New Pussycat?*, and was transcribed from a tape of the movie.

169: "The Scrolls," see note for page 92. "A Look at Organized

Crime" first appeared in *The New Yorker*, August 15, 1970, and was reprinted in *Getting Even*.

171: "Confessions of a Burglar," see note for page 27.

173: "Confessions of a Burglar," see note for page 27. "*Playboy* Interview: Woody Allen," see note for page 75.

174: "The Early Essays," see note for page 84.

Chapter Eight: My Philosophy: The Thing with Feathers

180: "By Destiny Denied," see note for page 164.

181: "Spring Bulletin," see note for page 52. "My Philosophy" first appeared in *The New Yorker*, December 27, 1969, and was reprinted in *Getting Even*. "The Condemned," see note for page 28.

185: "The Condemned," see note for page 28. "Examining Psychic Phenomena," see note for page 65.

188: "Consciousness Expanding Material" is excerpted from a much longer monologue entitled "Second Marriage," which was recorded live at Eugene's in San Francisco, August 1968, and first released on *The Third Woody Allen Album*. The monologue was later included on the two compilation albums. "The Early Essays," see note for page 84.

190: "The Condemned," see note for page 28. "Remembering Needleman," see note for page 64. "The Schmeed Memoirs" first appeared in *The New Yorker*, April 17, 1971, and was reprinted in *Getting Even*.

191: "My Speech to the Graduates" first appeared in *The New York Times*, August 10, 1979, and was reprinted in *Side Effects*. "The Condemned," see note for page 28.

193: "No Kaddish for Weinstein," see note for page 20.

196: *Death* (A Play) was first published in *Without Feathers*. A performance edition of the short play, entitled *Death*, was published by Samuel French in 1975. The play was later expanded into the 1992 movie, *Shadows and Fog*.

201: "My Speech to the Graduates," see note for page 191. "The Irish Genius," see note for page 27. "Selections from the Allen Notebooks," see note for page 33.

Chapter Nine: I Am Two with Nature

205: "A Moth Ate My Sports Jacket," is part of "The Great Renaldo" monologue, see note for page 78. "The Early Essays," see note for page 84. "My Speech to the Graduates," see note for page 191. "Selections from the Allen Notebooks," see note for page 33.

206: "The Lunatic's Tale," see note for page 85.

207: "The Early Essays," see note for page 84.

208: "The Early Essays," see note for page 84.

209: "A Guide to Some of the Lesser Ballets" first appeared in *The New Yorker*, October 28, 1972, and was reprinted in *Without Feathers*.

212: "I Shot a Moose Once" was

recorded live at the Shadows in Washington, D.C., April 1965, and released as "The Moose" on *Woody Allen, Volume 2,* and uncut on both compilation albums.

Chapter Ten: Religion: To God, I'm the Loyal Opposition

216: "Notes from the Overfed (After reading Dostoevski and the new *Weight Watchers* magazine on the same plane trip)" appeared in *The New Yorker,* March 16, 1968, and was later reprinted in *Getting Even.*

217: "Mr. Big," see note for page 54.

221: "The Scrolls," see note for page 92.

222: "My Speech to the Graduates," see note for page 191.

223: "Hassidic Tales, with a Guide to Their Interpretation by the Noted Scholar" first appeared in *The New Yorker,* June 20, 1970, and was reprinted in *Getting Even.*

224: "An Ethical Crisis" is part of "The Vodka Ad" monologue, which was recorded live at Eugene's in San Francisco, August 1968, and released on *The Third Woody Allen Album.* An edited version appears on both compilation albums.

226: "Remembering Needleman," see note for page 64.

229: "A Beserk Evangelist" is part of the "Bullet in My Breast Pocket" monologue, which was

recorded live at Mr. Kelly's in Chicago, March 1964, and later released on *Woody Allen* and both compilation albums. "Selections from the Allen Notebooks," see note for page 33.

231: "A Tremendous Religious Conflict" is part of the "NYU" monologue, which was recorded live at Mr. Kelly's in Chicago, March 1964, and released on *Woody Allen.* An edited version appears on both compilation albums.

233: "My Philosophy," see note for page 181.

234: "My Life Passed Before My Eyes" was recorded live at Eugene's in San Francisco, August 1968, and released as "Down South" on *The Third Woody Allen Album* and both compilation albums.

Chapter Eleven: Death Knocks!

241: "My Apology," see note for page 64. "My Philosophy," see note for page 181.

243: "I Just Can't Believe You're Death" is part of "Death Knocks (A Play)," which first appeared in *The New Yorker,* July 27, 1968, and was reprinted in *Getting Even.*

245: "Selections from the Allen Notebooks," see note for page 33. "The Condemned," see note for page 28.

249: "The Penalty" is an original short story that is being published for the first time in this book. "By Destiny Denied," see note for page 164. *Death* (A Play), see

note for page 196.

250: "Remembering Needleman," see note for page 64. *Death* (A Play), see note for page 196. "Not Dying" is a quote by Woody Allen from an unattributed interview.

252: "Reminiscences: Places and People," see note for page 15.

253: *Death* (A Play), see note for page 196.

255: "Examining Psychic Phenomena," see note for page 65. "The Condemned," see note for page 28.

257: "Examining Psychic Phenomena," see note for page 65. "The Lunatic's Tale," see note for page 85.

258: "Did He Suffer Much?" is part of a monologue entitled "Eggs Benedict," which was recorded lived at the Shadows in Washington, D.C., in April, 1965 and was released on *Woody Allen, Volume 2.* It appears in a somewhat edited version on both compilation albums. "Selections from the Allen Notebooks," see note for page 33. "Conversations with Helmholtz," see note for page 142.

259: "The *Rolling Stone* Interview: Woody Allen," see note for page 80.

Chapter Twelve: Things That Make Life Worth Living

271: "Fabulous Tales and Mythical Beasts," see note for page 59.

276: "One Great Regret " is

quoted from the author's biography on the dust jacket of *Getting Even*. "My Speech to the Graduates," see note for page 191. "Summing Up" was recorded live at Mr. Kelly's in Chicago, March 1964, and released on *Woody Allen* and both compilation albums.

Credits

Brian Hamill/Photoreporters: A great many of the photographs in this book are the work of Brian Hamill who has been shooting the still photographs on all of Woody Allen's movies since *Annie Hall* in 1977. The majority of these photos have not been previously published. Mr. Hamill's work appears on pages 2–3, 8–9, 12–13, 19, 20, 21, 28, 29, 31, 32, 34, 35, 38, 42, 44, 46, 47, 48, 49, 50, 53, 56, 58 (bottom), 72, 80, 81, 82–83, 86, 87, 88, 90, 92, 93, 94, 103, 106, 108, 114, 121, 122–123, 124, 125, 131, 133, 138, 139, 142–143 (middle), 146, 148, 149, 151, 154–155, 157, 158, 161, 167, 176–177, 182 (top), 189, 192, 194, 195, 197, 198, 202, 204, 206, 207, 211, 213, 214–215, 217, 236–237, 242, 243, 251, 256, 260–261, 262, 263, 276. Annotations on photos by Brian Hamill that appear in the text without captions are included below.

1: Photo by Philippe Halsman is from the archives of Rollins and Joffee, Inc. Copyright © Yvonne Halsman. This publicity still was used on the cover of *Getting Even*.

2–3: Portrait of Woody Allen taken by Brian Hamill/ Photoreporters in 1980.

5–7: All the photos that appear on these pages are from the interior text and are identified within their designated chapters with the following exception: pg. 6 (left, middle) photograph of Woody Allen and Mia Farrow by Brian Hamill/ Photoreporters was taken during the filming of *Crimes and Misdemeanors*, 1990.

Introduction: You Should Know That About Me

8–9: Portrait of Woody Allen taken by Brian Hamill/ Photoreporters during the filming of *Interiors*, 1978.

11: Still from a stand-up performance by Woody Allen at Mr. Kelly's in Chicago is from the archives of Rollins Joffee. Photographer unknown.

Chapter One: My Parents' Values: God and Carpeting

12–13: Photo by Brian Hamill/

Photoreporters was taken during the filming of *Radio Days*, 1987. The scene was eventually cut from the final edit of the film.

14: Mary Ellen Mark/Library.

16: Amusement Park, undated. Culver Pictures, Inc.

17: New York City subway, 1949. Culver Pictures, Inc.

18: Photograph from *Take the Money and Run*. Copyright © 1969 Capital Cities/ABC Inc.

19: Brian Hamill/Photoreporters. Taken during the filming of *Annie Hall*, this scene was cut from the final edit of the film.

22: Ellen Land-Weber, *The Passionate Collector*, 1980. Simon & Schuster.

23 and 25: Photograph from *Take the Money and Run*. Copyright © 1969 Capital Cities/ABC Inc.

26: Peter Lorre and Humphrey Bogart, *The Maltese Falcon*. Copyright © 1941 Turner

Entertainment Co. All Rights
Reserved.

34: This photograph of Irving
Selbst and Hope Sacharoff by
Brian Hamill/Photoreporters was
taken during the filming of *Radio
Days* but this scene was cut from
the final edit of the film.

36: Right and left: Immigrants,
New York City. Undated. Culver
Pictures, Inc.

37: Kaiser Wilhelm II. Copyright
© Photoreporters.

39: © Paperhouse Productions.

41: Van Gogh collage by Molly
Shields.

**Chapter Two: An
Unsentimental Education**

42: Photo by Brian Hamill/Photo-
reporters from *Annie Hall*, 1977.

55: Portrait of Woody Allen by
Jill Freedman, 1973.

**Chapter Three: Intellectuals
Only Kill Their Own**

56–57: Photo by Brian Hamill/
Photoreporters was taken during
the filming of *Stardust Memories*,
1980.

58: (Top) Saturn, as seen from the
Voyager mission spacecraft,
1981. NASA.

60: Christine Rodin, *Dresser*.

61: Jean-Paul Belmondo and Jean
Seberg, *Breathless*, 1959.

63: Culver Pictures, Inc.

64: Portrait of Albert Einstein ©
Paperhouse Productions. Courtesy of

The Hebrew University.

65: Portrait of Joseph Cotten
courtesy of Movie Star News.

**Chapter Four: New York vs.
Los Angeles**

66–67: The Brooklyn Bridge,
1951. Culver Pictures, Inc.

69: Mary Ellen Mark/Library.

70: Culver Pictures, Inc.

74: Roy Lichtenstein, *Electric
Cord*, oil on canvas, 28" x 18",
1961. © Roy Lichtenstein.
Courtesy Leo Castelli Gallery.

76: © Photoreporters.

77: Paul Duckworth, Fifth
Avenue, New York City.
© Photoreporters.

78: Max Weber, *Rush Hour, New
York*. Gift of the Avalon Founda-
tion, © 1992 National Gallery of
Art, Washington, 1915.

79: Photograph of Woody Allen
and Ed Sullivan was taken during
one of Woody Allen's frequent
appearances on "The Ed Sullivan
Show." Photographer unknown.
Still from the archives of Rollins
and Joffee.

**Chapter Five: Love: The
Good Sentimental**

82–83: Photo by Brian Hamill/
Photoreporters of Mia Farrow and
Alec Baldwin from *Alice*, 1990.

95: (Left) Grant Wood, American,
1892–1942, *American Gothic*, oil
on beaver board, 1930, Friends of
American Art Collection. The Art
Institute of Chicago. (Right)
Portrait of F. Scott and Zelda

Fitzgerald taken in May, 1923, is
from Culver Pictures, Inc.

97: Mary Ellen Mark/Library.

107: Walter Sittig. © Nouvelles
Images S. A. éditeurs et Voller
Ernst 1991.

110: Paul Klee, *Comedians'
Handbill*, 1938. Gouache on
newsprint on light cardboard.
Metropolitan Museum of Art, The
Berggruen Klee Collection, 1984.

112: Great white shark is © 1991
Ron and Valerie Taylor.
Reprinted with permission of
Ardea London Ltd.

116–117: Robert Mihovil ©
1986. Photoreporters.

119: Marc Chagall, *Double
Portrait with Wine Glass*,
1917–18. Paris, Musée National
d'Art Moderne. Credit: Scala/Art
Resource, New York.

**Chapter Six: These Modern
Analysts!**

122–123: Photo by Brian
Hamill/Photoreporters was taken
during the filming of *Stardust
Memories*, 1980.

127: Photographer unknown.
Photo from the Rollins and Joffee
archives.

128: The Trojan Horse, woodcut,
1632. Culver Pictures, Inc.

129: The Brain. © The
Dreamland Collection.

134: Edvard Munch, *The Scream*,
1893. Copyright Oslo Kommunes
Kunstsamlinger. Munch Museet.
O.K.K. Reg. nr:514.

137: Sigmund Freud, April, 1932. Culver Pictures, Inc.

140–141: Pilgrimage to Lourdes, February, 1958. Photographer unknown. Copyright © Photoreporters.

142: Portrait of Woody Allen is from the archives of Rollins and Joffee, Inc. Photographer unknown.

Chapter Seven: Work, Art and Funnier Jokes

144–145: Charlie Chaplin, *Modern Times*, 1936. Culver Pictures, Inc.

148: Brian Hamill portrait of Mollie Regan was cut from the final edit of *Radio Days*.

151: Brian Hamill photograph of Woody Allen and Juliette Lewis was taken during a scene that was cut from the final edit of *Husbands and Wives*.

152: Pablo Picasso, *Gertrude Stein*, 1906. Oil on canvas. Metropolitan Museum of Art. Bequest of Gertrude Stein, 1946.

153: Ernest Hemingway and Antonio Ordoñez, ca. late 1950s. © Photoreporters.

163: Greg Wakabayashi, *Blueprint: Plan, Elevation, and Axonometric Views of the Sandwich*, 1993.

165: *Hercules Supporting the Celestial Sphere*. Detail from the Sphere series. Woven by or at the order of Georg Wezeler, after a cartoon attributed to Bernaert van Orley. Brussels, ca. 1520–1530. Royal Palace, Madrid.

170–171: Woolworth's, 1942. Culver Pictures, Inc.

172: Photograph from *Take the Money and Run*. Copyright © 1969 Capital Cities/ABC Inc.

174: New York City market. Undated. Culver Pictures, Inc.

175: Cash register illustration from an ad for Champion Cash Register, 1884. Culver Pictures, Inc.

Chapter Eight: My Philosophy: The Thing with Feathers

176–177: Photograph by Brian Hamill taken during the filming of *Manhattan*, 1979.

178–179: "The Famous Skating Sextette" at Thos. Healy's Crystal Carnival Ice Rink. Undated. Culver Pictures, Inc.

181: Mark Gabor, *Steak at Lena's*, 1992.

182: Jackson Pollock, 1912–1956, *Untitled* (ca. 1939–42). India ink on paper (double-sided). Purchase, with funds from the Julia B. Engle Purchase Fund and Drawing Committee. Collection of the Whitney Museum of Art, New York. Photo by Geoffrey Clements, New York. © 1992.

184: Mary Ellen Mark/Library.

187: Gustav Klimt, Werkvorlage zum Stoclet-Fries, *"DIE ERWARTUNG,"* 1905/7.

201. Portrait of Emily Dickinson (1830–1886) is from Culver Pictures, Inc.

Chapter Nine: I Am Two with Nature

202–203: Photograph by Brian Hamill/Photoreporters of Diane Keaton and Woody Allen from *Annie Hall*, 1977.

208: René Magritte, *The Third Dimension*, 1942.

Chapter Ten: Religion: To God, I'm the Loyal Opposition

214–215: Photograph by Brian Hamill/Photoreporters of Woody Allen, Fred Gwynne and Steven Keats, was taken during the filming of *Shadows and Fog*, 1991.

218: Marc Chagall, *Remembrance*, ca. 1918. Gouache, India ink and pencil on paper. Solomon R. Guggenheim Museum, New York, Gift, Solomon R. Guggenheim, 1941. Photo: David Heald copyright The Solomon R. Guggenheim Foundation, New York.

221: Decorative doors of the Ark of the Torah Scroll, Italy, 19th century. New York Public Library.

223: Culver Pictures, Inc.

225: Marc Chagall, French, born Russia, 1887–1985, *The Praying Jew*, oil on canvas, 1923 copy of a 1914 work, 116.9 x 88.9 cm, Joseph Winterbotham Collection, 1937.188. Photograph © 1992, The Art Institute of Chicago. All Rights Reserved.

226: On location with the crew from *Bananas*, 1971. Photo by Jack Stager from the archives of Rollins and Joffee, Inc.

229: Remington portable. Undated. Culver Pictures, Inc.

230: Culver Pictures, Inc.

232: *Aaron the High Priest Filling the Menorah*. Hebrew manuscript, late 13th century. ©1977 The British Library Board.

234: Inauguration of Master Simeon Marcus as a member of the Holy House of Israel, *Leslie's Illustrated News*, April 28, 1877. Culver Pictures, Inc.

235: Pentateuch, written about 3200 years ago. *Leslie's Illustrated News*. Culver Pictures, Inc.

Chapter Eleven: Death Knocks!

236–237: Photograph by Brian Hamill/Photoreporters of Michael Kirby taken during the filming of *Shadows and Fog*, 1991.

239: Tarot card from the Visconti-Sforza, attributed to Bonifacio Bembo, ca. mid-15th century. New York Public Library.

240: Jacques-Louis David, *The Death of Socrates*, 1787. Culver Pictures, Inc.

246 and 249: Parrot drawings by Greg Wakabayashi, 1993.

252: *Book of the Dead of Khensmose*, Ägyptische Kunst, (21. Dynastie, 11.–10. Jh.v.Chr.) © 1989 by Kunsthistorisches Museum, Wien.

254: Christine Rodin, *Cemetery*.

Chapter Twelve: Things That Make Life Worth Living

260: Photograph by Brian Hamill/Photoreporters of Marshall Brickman and Woody Allen at Michael's Pub, New York City, 1976.

264: Portrait of Marlon Brando. Courtesy of Movie Star News.

264: Portrait of Louis Armstrong, taken in New York City, 1966, by Philippe Halsman.Copyright © Yvonne Halsman.

264: Paul Cézanne, French, 1829–1906, *The Basket of Apples*, oil on canvas, ca. 1895, 65.5 x 81.3 cm, Helen Birch Bartlett Memorial Collection, 1926.252. Photograph © 1992 The Art Institute of Chicago. All Rights Reserved.

265: Portrait of Willie Mays Copyright © 1990 TV Sports Mailbag.

265: Groucho Marx. With permission of the Marx estate.

267: Humphrey Bogart, *To Have and Have Not*. © 1945 Turner Entertainment Co. All Rights Reserved.

269: Photograph by Mary Ellen Mark/Library of Woody Allen and Mia Farrow taken during the filming of *Shadows and Fog*, 1991.

271: Max Ernst, *Sorcellerie Ou Quelque Farce Macabre*. New York Public Library.

273: Chico, Harpo and Groucho Marx, *At the Circus*. © 1939 Turner Entertainment Co. All Rights Reserved.

274: Photograph of Radio City Music Hall, Rockefeller Center, New York City, is reprinted from an antique postcard, undated.

275: Photograph of Essex Street on the Lower East Side of New York City, 1945. Culver Pictures, Inc.

Acknowledgments

"Right now it's only a notion, but I think I can get money to make it into a concept, and later turn it into an idea."

Annie Hall

Working on this book has been a rewarding and enriching experience, mainly because of the many talented people who were responsible for turning this notion into a book. My thanks to:

Linda Kirland at Rollins & Joffe, Inc., who was the first champion of this project.

Jack Rollins, who took me into the family and steered the course from start to finish.

Nai Chang, who brought his classic sense of style and design to this book, and, as always, was extremely generous with his time and talent.

Sarah Lazin, an agent like you shouldn't know from, who defines grace under pressure and provided infinite patience and continuing encouragement.

Jonathan Segal, a champion editor, consummate professional and, like me, a true advocate.

Ernie Boehm of Photoreporters who graciously allowed me free reign in his office where I spent many, many hours reviewing all of Brian Hamill's contact sheets.

Kristen Dolan, an incredibly talented researcher, tackled a difficult and complicated task with a creative eye.

Many people at Knopf were instrumental in shepherding this project: Sonny Mehta, Carol Janeway, Katherine Hourigan, Mel Rosenthal, Michael Graves, Carey Guidice, Lauri del Commune, Amy Capen, Elise Solomon, Andy Hughes, Carol Devine Carson, Chip Kidd, and, especially, Ida Giragossian.

Lauren Gibson at Manhattan Film Center and Irwin J. Tenenbaum of Sinclair Tenenbaum & Co., Inc., were also very helpful.

And, finally, a personal thanks to Mark, Mark and Mark for pulling me through.

Linda Sunshine

Index